I0605283

코리아

COOK KOREA!

BILLY LAW

Anyoung Haseyo!

Hello!

I HAD MY FIRST REAL TASTE OF KOREAN FOOD AT A FRIEND'S BIRTHDAY DINNER IN A TRADITIONAL KOREAN BARBECUE RESTAURANT – AND I FELL HARD FOR IT. NOT JUST THE FLAVOURS, BUT THE WHOLE EXPERIENCE. TEN OF US WERE GATHERED AROUND A CHARCOAL GRILL SET INTO THE MIDDLE OF THE TABLE, SURROUNDED BY AN ASTONISHING ARRAY OF SLICED MEATS, FRESH VEGETABLES AND SPICY SAUCES AND MARINADES. IT WAS HOT, SMOKY AND NOISY – AND I WAS IN HEAVEN!

Everyone around the table was a little flushed, fanning themselves with menus, turning the meat with tongs and downing cold beers all at the same time. I could feel the heat from the grill on my face, aromatic smoke lingered in the air, and meat juices sizzled noisily on the smouldering coals. This was a real communal meal – with a sense of teamwork and excitement because we all played our own small parts in the cooking. And, of course, those slices of grilled meat – juicy, hot and spicy, crispy with caramelised marinade and imbued with the smoky flavour of the charcoal – were just as delicious as anticipated!

Since that day, my love of 'Seoul food' has grown into an obsession with every element of Korean cuisine. And those elements are varied and ever-changing: from the vibrant street-food scene, to the traditional hotpots, from the irresistible bar snacks, to the formidable range of trademark fermented kimchi.

Because it's in the kitchens of Korea that fermentation – practised for around 2000 years as a method of preserving food – has been raised and perfected to an art form. Kimchi is the well-known spicy fermented sidekick to every meal, and perhaps the first dish that comes to mind when you think of Korean food in general. While cabbage kimchi has become a global superstar in recent years, there are actually more than 150 variations on the kimchi recipe – and the number is growing constantly, which says a lot about the importance of this beloved dish.

Kimchi sits at the very heart of the country's food culture, and it's easy and incredibly rewarding to make. Set aside a weekend afternoon and get your friends over for some batch cooking. It's also extremely addictive – a good thing, now that we all know how great fermented

food is for our gut health. I predict that, when you've made it once, you'll never again be without a few jars of this umami-packed goodness in your fridge. You'll also discover how to turn it into the ultimate comfort-food soup, irresistible crispy fritters and a few different hotpots – now that's versatility!

Korean cooking runs an impressive range from that exciting communal barbecue grill to the simplest of home-cooked meals – there's a real mastery of tasty soups and traditional stews made with very few ingredients and little fuss but a lot of flavour. And let's not forget the famously spicy, crunchy 'beer snacks' and array of iconic can't-walk-past-it street foods.

As well as piping-hot pancakes, nostalgic goldfish bread and mountains of shaved ice topped with sweet red bean paste, that ever-evolving street-food menu includes the only KFC anyone should be eating: Korean fried chicken! I love fried chicken in any form, but Korean fried chicken has raised crunch to a whole new level. I've included four variations on the recipe here, so you can all become as addicted as I am!

Something that sets traditional home-style Korean cooking apart from other cuisines is the number of different banchan (side dishes) that accompany any meal. An array of steamed, stir-fried, marinated or sauteed veggies – from refreshingly spicy cucumber salad to stir-fried radish or soy-braised potatoes – add crunch or silky texture, spice and flavour to every dinnertime. Even the humblest kitchen supper might include three banchan, while the tables of Korea's ancient royal kings would have been laden with up to 12. Leftover banchan in your fridge? There's a perfect recipe for that: the famously comforting and colourful bibimbap will turn those leftovers into an effortless feast.

It's been an epic and completely delicious journey writing this cookbook, from researching the recipes, to cooking and testing every single dish. You should have seen my fridge – every inch packed with different containers of fermenting kimchi! And now I'm incredibly excited and grateful to share it all with you. (Not the kimchi, sorry – I'm keeping that for myself!)

KAMSAHAMNIDA!
(Thank you!)

김치김치
Ki

mchi

KIMCHI IS BELOVED. THIS HUMBLE DISH OF FERMENTED VEGETABLES SITS AT THE VERY HEART OF KOREA'S FOOD CULTURE. IT'S THE TRADITIONAL SPICY SIDEKICK THAT'S SERVED WITH ALMOST EVERY MEAL; A STAPLE IN EVERY KITCHEN, WHICH HAS WOVEN ITSELF INTO THE TRADITIONS OF DAILY LIFE. KOREANS HAVE RAISED THE ANCIENT TECHNIQUE OF FERMENTATION TO AN ART FORM, AND KIMCHI IS THE NATIONAL EMBODIMENT OF THAT ACHIEVEMENT. NOW THAT WE'RE ALL AWARE OF HEALTHY PROBIOTICS, IT'S A GOOD EXCUSE TO KEEP YOUR FRIDGE WELL STOCKED.

AND, POPULAR AS IT MIGHT BE, KIMCHI ISN'T JUST MADE WITH CABBAGE – THERE ARE HUNDREDS OF VARIETIES USING DIFFERENT VEGETABLES. SOME ARE BEST LEFT FOR WEEKS TO FERMENT; OTHERS CAN BE EATEN STRAIGHTAWAY. WHICHEVER KIMCHI YOU CHOOSE TO MAKE, THIS IS 'SEOUL FOOD' AT ITS VERY BEST!

Cabbage kimchi

Baechu kimchi

Of the hundreds of varieties of kimchi, napa (Chinese) cabbage kimchi is the most popular. Almost every household has a jar of cabbage kimchi sitting in the fridge or cool cellar, fermenting away happily. And every family has their own closely guarded secret recipe. Now I'm going to throw mine into the kimchi jar!

Don't be intimidated by the length of this recipe: kimchi is easy and straightforward to make, but allow at least half a day in the kitchen to really savour the experience. This is weekend batch-cooking at its best. There are six stages: salting the cabbage; turning; rinsing; marinating; rubbing the chilli paste onto the cabbage; and fermentation. Ideally, the cabbage should be left to ferment for at least two weeks. It's a waiting game, but the rewards are worth it.

MAKES ABOUT 2.5 KG (5½ LB)

- 1 NAPA (CHINESE) CABBAGE (ABOUT 2 KG/4 LB 6 OZ)
- 315 G (1 CUP) COARSE COOKING SALT
- 450 G (1 LB) KOREAN RADISH OR DAIKON, PEELED
- 4 SPRING ONIONS (SCALLIONS)

KIMCHI CHILLI PASTE

- CLOVES FROM 1 GARLIC BULB (ABOUT 10), PEELED
- 2 CM (¾ IN) PIECE OF GINGER, PEELED
- 1 ONION, QUARTERED
- 65 G (½ CUP) GOCHUGARU
- 125 ML (½ CUP) FISH SAUCE
- 1 TABLESPOON CASTER (SUPERFINE) SUGAR

First, make the kimchi chilli paste. Put the garlic, ginger and onion in a blender or food processor and blend on high speed to form a fine paste. Transfer to a large mixing bowl.

Add the gochugaru, fish sauce and sugar, and stir until the sugar has dissolved. Use immediately or store in an airtight container in the fridge for up to 2 weeks.

Salting

Halve the cabbage lengthways from root to tip. Cut each half in half again so that you end up with quarters. Give the cabbage segments a quick wash and tease the leaves apart gently from the core, being careful not to tear them, and rinse to remove any dirt. Shake off any excess water and set aside.

Working with one quarter at a time, place the cabbage on a flat surface with the outermost leaf on the bottom. You will need 80 g (¼ cup) salt per quarter. Starting from the bottom leaf, generously sprinkle salt over the thickest parts of the cabbage, using less salt on the leafy parts. Place the salted cabbage segment in a large mixing bowl. Repeat with the remaining cabbage and salt.

Once all the cabbage segments are salted and sitting in the bowl (stack them on top of each other if necessary), pour in 1 litre (4 cups) of water. Press down to ensure the segments are completely covered, then set aside to pickle for 4–6 hours. ›

EQUIPMENT

1 × 12 LITRE (12½ QUART) STAINLESS STEEL MIXING BOWL

1 LARGE COLANDER

1 PAIR OF FOOD PREPARATION GLOVES

1 × 4 LITRE (4 QUART) AIRTIGHT CONTAINER

4 × 475 ML (16 FL OZ) STERILISED MASON JARS WITH LIDS (OPTIONAL)

NOTE / The kimchi keeps well in the fridge for a minimum of 1-2 months. If it begins to taste sour, use it to make Kimchi fried rice (page 108), Kimchi pancakes with pork belly (page 84) or Kimchi stew (page 149). If it has turned mouldy and fizzy, discard it.

Turning
Every 1–2 hours, rotate the cabbage segments to ensure each piece is thoroughly coated in the pickling liquid. The cabbage is ready when the thickest parts are soft and bendable.

Rinsing
Thoroughly rinse the cabbage under cold running water three times. Squeeze each segment to remove as much water as possible then transfer to a colander, cut side down, to drip-dry.

Marinating the radish
Cut the radish into matchsticks about 5 mm (¼ in) wide and 5 cm (2 in) long. Place in a large bowl. Cut the spring onions into 2.5 cm (1 in) lengths and add to the bowl. Add the kimchi chilli paste and stir until well combined. Set aside for 1 hour to marinate. After an hour, the radish will have softened and you should have a loose, wet paste.

Rubbing
Transfer the cabbage segments, cut side up, to a baking tray. Working with one segment at a time, spread one-quarter of the radish chilli paste evenly over and in between the cabbage leaves, starting from the outermost leaf. Wear food preparation gloves if necessary to protect your hands from the chilli.

Once the cabbage is well coated in the chilli paste, fold the leaf part of the cabbage over towards the stem to form a nicely wrapped parcel. Pack each parcel, cut side down, snugly into an airtight container,

Rinse the baking tray with 60 ml (¼ cup) of water to loosen any leftover chilli paste. Add any loose cabbage leaves to the tray, stir briefly, then pour everything into one container over the cabbage segments. Seal the container with a lid.

Fermentation
Place the container in a cool spot away from direct sunlight and leave to ferment for 2 days. The kimchi will ferment more quickly during summer and more slowly during the cooler months.

After 2 days, pack each cabbage segment into a mason jar, seal tightly, and store in the fridge. The kimchi will be ready to eat after 2 days, but the flavours will continue to develop the longer it is stored.

To serve
When you are ready to eat, remove the kimchi from the jar. Use a pair of kitchen scissors to cut off as many leaves as you want, then return the remaining cabbage to the jar. Cut the kimchi into 2.5 cm (1 in) pieces to serve.

간장

Radish kimchi

Kkakdugi

I love these cubes of pickled radish – they're spicy and tangy with a great crunch, and the perfect match for fried food such as KFC (page 88). Like all kimchi, the flavour of this radish version continues to develop over the course of its fermentation. It starts off vibrant and fresh with a pungent aroma from the fish sauce, then mellows after a few weeks as the sweetness of the radish starts to come through. As it continues to mature, the fermentation will transform the sugar to acid, giving the kimchi that distinctive tanginess and sharp taste.

MAKES ABOUT 1 KG (2 LB 3 OZ)

- 1 KG (2 LB 3 OZ) KOREAN RADISH OR DAIKON, PEELED
- 2 TABLESPOONS COARSE COOKING SALT
- 1 TABLESPOON CASTER (SUPERFINE) SUGAR
- 5-6 GARLIC CLOVES, CRUSHED
- 2 CM (¾ IN) PIECE OF GINGER, PEELED AND FINELY CHOPPED
- 30 G (¼ CUP) GOCHUGARU
- 125 ML (½ CUP) FISH SAUCE

Cut the radish into 2 cm (¾ in) cubes and place in a large bowl. Add the salt and sugar and mix well. Set aside to pickle for 30 minutes, then drain and return the radish to the bowl.

Add the garlic, ginger, gochugaru and fish sauce and mix, using your hands, until the radish is well coated.

Fill a few sterilised glass jars with the kimchi. Press down to remove any air bubbles, then seal the jars with tight-fitting lids. Store the jars in a cool place away from direct sunlight and leave to ferment for 2 days. Transfer to the fridge and store for up to 1 month.

RADISH KIMCHI

Radish water kimchi

Dongchimi

Dongchimi (radish water kimchi) is not your typical kimchi. This mild soup is not only tasty, but the fermentation produces good bacteria that promote digestion. A bowl of dongchimi is usually served as an appetiser and palate cleanser before a meal. The tangy broth can also be used as the soup base for Chilled buckwheat noodle soup (page 126).

Dongchimi is typically made in late autumn when radishes (preferably small baby radishes) are in season and at their peak flavour and sweetness. Then it's left to ferment for several weeks, ready to be eaten during the cold winter months.

MAKES 1 × 6 LITRE (6 QUART) JAR

- 1 × 2 KG (4 LB 6 OZ) KOREAN RADISH OR DAIKON, PEELED (SEE NOTE)
- 80 G (¼ CUP) COARSE COOKING SALT
- 6-8 GARLIC CLOVES, THINLY SLICED
- ½ ONION, THINLY SLICED
- 3 SPRING ONIONS (SCALLIONS), CUT INTO 10 CM (4 IN) LENGTHS
- 4 GREEN CHILLIES, TRIMMED AND CUT INTO THIN STRIPS
- 1 NASHI OR ASIAN PEAR, UNPEELED, WASHED

Cut the radish crossways into four equal portions. Cut each portion into quarters.

Transfer to a large mixing bowl. Sprinkle the salt over the radish and toss to coat with your hands. Leave to sit for 30–40 minutes, until the radish has softened and released some of its liquid. Drain the liquid into a jug using a fine-mesh sieve.

Put the salted radish into one 6 litre (6 quart) sterilised glass jar or two smaller jars, then top with the garlic, onion, spring onion, green chilli and, finally, the pear.

Mix together 2.25 litres (2¼ quarts) of water with the reserved pickling liquid and pour into the jar. Seal tightly, and ferment at room temperature away from direct sunlight for 2 days. After 2 days, taste the liquid and adjust the seasoning accordingly. If it's too salty, add more water. If it's not salty enough, add more salt and stir to dissolve. Leave to ferment for another day and taste again. It should be a little salty, sweet, sour, garlicky and hot from the chillies. Once you are happy with the flavours, transfer the jar to the fridge and chill before serving. It will keep in the fridge for up to 1 month.

Serve one piece of radish per portion. Take the radish out of the jar and slice thinly. Place the sliced radish in a small soup bowl and top with some of the garlic, onion, spring onion and chilli. Give the liquid in the jar a quick stir, then ladle some of the liquid over the radish and serve chilled.

NOTE / Most Korean radishes are quite large, and must be sliced in order to fit in a jar. If you can find small ones, just pickle the whole radish without peeling. Whole pickled radishes will keep longer than sliced radishes.

Stuffed cucumber kimchi

Oi sobagi

Deliciously crunchy and refreshing, this is a perfect summertime snack and great for anyone who loves pickled cucumbers. Oi sobagi ferments relatively quickly compared to other types of kimchi and doesn't keep as well – so, best make just enough for one meal and enjoy it straightaway.

MAKES ABOUT 1 KG (2 LB 3 OZ)

- 1 KG (2 LB 3 OZ) SHORT CUCUMBERS
- 2 TABLESPOONS COARSE COOKING SALT
- ½ QUANTITY × GARLIC CHIVE KIMCHI (PAGE 30)
- 1 ONION, THINLY SLICED

Wash the cucumbers and shake off any excess water. Top and tail the cucumbers, then cut in half crossways. Stand the cucumbers upright and slice lengthways into quarters, stopping about 1 cm (½ in) short of the base so the quarters are still attached at the base. Transfer to a large mixing bowl and set aside.

Add 1 litre (4 cups) of water to a large saucepan and bring to a rolling boil over high heat. Add the salt and stir until dissolved. Remove from the heat and pour the hot salted water over the cucumbers. Put a small plate over the cucumbers to keep them fully submerged and leave to steep for 2 hours. Drain, and rinse the cucumbers in cold water twice.

Cut the garlic chive kimchi into 2 cm (¾ in) lengths, then add to the cucumbers with the onion. Using your hands, massage the mixture until the cucumbers are thoroughly coated.

Stuff each cucumber half with about 1 tablespoon of the garlic chive kimchi. Press the cucumber quarters together to secure the kimchi inside, then transfer to an airtight container.

Enjoy the stuffed cucumber kimchi straightaway.

01 / RADISH KIMCHI 02 / CABBAGE KIMCHI 03 / STUFFED CUCUMBER KIMCHI

04 / RADISH WATER KIMCHI 05 / SPRING ONION KIMCHI 06 / GARLIC CHIVE KIMCHI

Spring onion kimchi

Pa kimchi

Not all kimchi takes time to prepare and ferment. This spring onion version is particularly simple and can be eaten immediately. Young spring onions are best here – the sort that are soft, green, skinny and sweet, rather than the fat, tougher stalks. This recipe is also perfect for using up any almost-wilted spring onions that might be languishing in your fridge. I think that's a great rule for life – don't throw it away; make kimchi instead!

MAKES ABOUT 350 G (12½ OZ)

300 G (10½ OZ) SPRING ONIONS (SCALLIONS)

50 G (¼ CUP) KIMCHI CHILLI PASTE (PAGE 16)

Wash the spring onions thoroughly to get rid of any dirt, then shake off the excess water. Trim the root ends and any wilted leaves.

Transfer the spring onions to a baking tray and add the chilli paste. Using your hands, rub the chilli paste all over the spring onions until well coated.

Eat straightaway or leave the kimchi to ferment at room temperature in an airtight container for 1–2 days, then refrigerate for 2–3 weeks.

To serve, grab a bunch of spring onions and cut them into 5–10 cm (2–4 in) lengths. Serve as a side dish.

Garlic chive kimchi

Buchu kimchi

Just like spring onion kimchi (page 28), this garlic chive version doesn't need fermentation and can be eaten straightaway – it's refreshingly good for cutting through rich meat dishes, such as Stir-fried spicy pork (page 98). Make this during spring and summer, when garlic chives are in abundance.

MAKES 550 G (1 LB 3 OZ)

450 G (1 LB) GARLIC CHIVES

100 G (½ CUP) KIMCHI CHILLI PASTE (PAGE 16)

TOASTED SESAME SEEDS, TO SERVE

Put the garlic chives in a large bowl and cover with water. Gently shake to remove any dirt stuck between the leaves. Drain, and repeat. Shake off any excess water.

Return the chives to the bowl, and add the kimchi chilli paste. Using your hands, gently rub the paste over the chives to evenly coat them. Leave to stand at room temperature for 2–3 hours, until the chives have marinated and softened. Eat straightaway or store in an airtight container in the fridge for up to 1 month.

When you're ready to serve, cut the chives into 5 cm (2 in) lengths. Sprinkle with toasted sesame seeds and serve as a side dish.

Street Food

거리 음식

KOREA'S VIBRANT STREET-FOOD CULTURE IS CONSTANTLY EVOLVING – SO MUCH SO THAT IT'S OFTEN REFERRED TO AS A 'MOVING RESTAURANT'. DISHES THAT WERE ONCE ONLY MADE IN ANCIENT ROYAL PALACES GRADUALLY FIND THEIR WAY TO THE STREET-FOOD STALLS, THEN OFTEN ENTER THE MAINSTREAM AS A FAMILY MEAL. THE OLDEST MARKETS OPENED IN THE 1400S, WITH A HUGE MODERN RESURGENCE IN STREET FOODS DURING THE 1960S.

NIGHT MARKETS, FOOD TRUCKS AND STREET-VENDOR STALLS ALL OFFER UP A DAZZLING RANGE OF THE CRUNCHY, SALTY, SOUPY, SPICY AND SWEET – FROM THE TRADITIONAL TTEOKBOKKI AND GOLDFISH BREAD THAT ARE FOUND ON EVERY STREET CORNER, TO CRAZY TORNADO POTATO HOTDOG STICKS.

SOME OF THE SWEETS IN THIS CHAPTER ARE RELATIVELY NEW INVENTIONS, WITH FUSION INGREDIENTS AND FLAVOURS THAT HAVE TAKEN THE STREET-FOOD SCENE BY STORM, WHILE OTHERS ARE TRADITIONAL CLASSICS, LOVED FOR GENERATIONS, THAT INDULGE A NOSTALGIA FOR CHILDHOOD. THERE ARE SO MANY REASONS TO EAT STREET!

SFC
BIO
Sparkling

Traditional spicy rice cakes

Tteokbokki

Tteokbokki is for sale on nearly every street corner in Korea – it's a hugely comforting and soul-satisfying street food that's beloved across the country. This recipe – stir-fried chewy rice cakes and fish cakes doused in a deep-red spicy sauce – is for a very typical, traditional tteokbokki, using inexpensive ingredients. Early versions of the dish date all the way back to the 1400s, and it re-emerged onto the scene in the late 1960s.

SERVES 4–6

- 500 G (1 LB 2 OZ) FROZEN TTEOK (KOREAN TUBULAR RICE CAKES)
- 1 TABLESPOON OLIVE OIL
- 500 ML (2 CUPS) VEGETABLE STOCK
- 2 KOREAN FISH CAKE SHEETS, CUT INTO BITE-SIZED PIECES (SEE NOTE)
- 2 SPRING ONIONS (SCALLIONS), CUT INTO 5 CM (2 IN) LENGTHS
- TOASTED SESAME SEEDS, TO SERVE

TTEOKBOKKI SAUCE

- 3 GARLIC CLOVES, MINCED
- 2 TABLESPOONS GOCHUGARU
- 100 G (⅓ CUP) GOCHUJANG
- 1 TABLESPOON SOY SAUCE
- 1 TABLESPOON SUGAR
- 2 TEASPOONS SESAME OIL

Separate the frozen tteok into individual pieces, then soak them in warm water for 20 minutes to soften. Drain, then place the tteok in a bowl and toss with the olive oil until well coated so they don't stick together.

Pour the vegetable stock into a large deep frying pan over medium–high heat. Add the tteokbokki sauce ingredients, stir well to combine and bring to the boil. Add the tteok and cook, stirring frequently, for 8–10 minutes, until the tteok is very soft and the sauce is reduced and thick.

Add the fish cake pieces to the pan, then reduce the heat to medium and simmer for 5 minutes. Taste and adjust the seasoning if needed. Add the spring onion, give everything a final stir, then transfer the stew to a serving dish. Sprinkle sesame seeds over the top and serve immediately.

NOTE / You can also add thin slices of fish cake to the dish.

Pan-fried spicy rice cakes

Gireum tteokbokki

Although tteokbokki is traditionally served in a spicy chilli sauce with fish cakes and other ingredients (page 37), I also love this simple, sauceless version that's made by pan-frying the rice cakes to a lovely caramelised crisp finish. The flavour is intensified and the crispy–chewy rice cake is utterly satisfying, especially on a chilly day.

SERVES 4

- 500 G (1 LB 2 OZ) FROZEN TTEOK (KOREAN TUBULAR RICE CAKES)
- 1½ TABLESPOONS OLIVE OIL
- 2 GARLIC CLOVES, FINELY CHOPPED
- 2 TABLESPOONS GOCHUGARU
- 70 G (¼ CUP) GOCHUJANG
- 2 TABLESPOONS SOY SAUCE
- 1 TABLESPOON CASTER (SUPERFINE) SUGAR
- 2 TEASPOONS SESAME OIL
- PINCH OF FRESHLY GROUND BLACK PEPPER
- 1 SPRING ONION (SCALLION), THINLY SLICED
- 2 TEASPOONS TOASTED SESAME SEEDS

Bring a large saucepan of water to the boil over medium–high heat. Add the tteok and cook for 3 minutes or until soft. Drain, then transfer the rice cakes to a large bowl and drizzle with 1 tablespoon of the olive oil. Mix well to stop the tteok sticking together, then set aside.

Combine the garlic, gochugaru, gochujang, soy sauce, sugar, sesame oil and black pepper in a small bowl, and mix well. Pour the mixture over the tteok and stir until they are well coated in the marinade. Cover with plastic wrap and leave to marinate at room temperature for at least 1 hour.

Heat the remaining olive oil in a large non-stick frying pan over medium–high heat. Working in small batches, fry the marinated tteok for 2–3 minutes, until crispy and slightly charred. Turn the tteok frequently so they don't stick to the pan. Toss in the spring onion and sesame seeds, give it a quick stir, then dish up.

Korean corn dogs 3 ways

Gamja-hotdogs

The classic hotdog sausage on a stick, coated in thick batter and deep-fried, has become a worldwide fairground favourite over the past few decades. Corn dog, dagwood dog, dippy dog, pluto pup, pogo – call it what you like, they've all got the same vital ingredients. If you're a fan, you'll love these street-food versions. The Korean corn dog is definitely king of the dogs!

SERVES 4

- 4 HOTDOG FRANKFURTERS
- KETCHUP, TO SERVE
- MUSTARD, TO SERVE

POLENTA BATTER

- 150 G (1 CUP) PLAIN (ALL-PURPOSE) FLOUR
- 75 G (½ CUP) POLENTA (CORNMEAL)
- 2 TEASPOONS CASTER (SUPERFINE) SUGAR
- PINCH OF SALT
- ½ TEASPOON BAKING SODA
- 1 LARGE EGG
- 250 ML (1 CUP) MILK
- VEGETABLE OIL, FOR DEEP-FRYING

To make the polenta batter, combine the flour, polenta, sugar, salt and baking soda in a large bowl. Add the egg and milk and stir to create a thick, loose batter. If the batter is too thick or dries up, add some water and stir well. Pour the batter into a tall, narrow vessel deep enough to dip each frankfurter into, such as a deep tumbler glass or water bottle.

Insert a bamboo skewer lengthways through each frankfurter and set aside.

Half-fill a deep-fryer or a deep, wide heavy-based saucepan or sturdy wok with vegetable oil. Heat the oil to 180°C (350°F) over medium–high heat.

Now continue with your choice of the corn dog variations opposite.

FRENCH FRIES HOTDOGS

- 75 G (½ CUP) PLAIN (ALL-PURPOSE) FLOUR, FOR DUSTING
- HANDFUL OF FROZEN CRINKLE-CUT FRENCH FRIES, THAWED, CUT INTO 1 CM (½ INCH) CUBES

Spread the flour in a shallow tray, and the chopped fries in a second tray.

Dredge one of the frankfurters in the flour, shaking off the excess. Dip it in the batter until fully coated, allowing the excess batter to drip off, then roll it in the fries, ensuring they completely stick to the batter.

Immediately lower the hotdog into the hot oil and fry for 5–7 minutes, until golden brown. Remove and place on a wire rack with paper towel underneath to catch the excess oil. One at a time, coat and cook the remaining frankfurters in the same way.

Serve hot, with ketchup and mustard.

FRIED BREAD HOTDOGS

- 75 G (½ CUP) PLAIN (ALL-PURPOSE) FLOUR, FOR DUSTING
- 4 SLICES DAY-OLD BREAD, CUT INTO 1 CM (½ INCH) CUBES

Spread the flour in a shallow tray, and the bread cubes in a second tray.

Dredge one of the frankfurters in the flour, shaking off the excess. Dip it in the batter until fully coated, allowing the excess batter to drip off, then roll it in the bread cubes until fully covered.

Immediately lower the hotdog into the hot oil and fry for 5–7 minutes, until golden brown. Remove and place on a wire rack with paper towel underneath to catch the excess oil. One at a time, coat and cook the remaining frankfurters in the same way.

Serve hot, with ketchup and mustard.

PANKO CHEESE HOTDOGS

- 4 SLICES WHITE BREAD, CRUSTS REMOVED
- 60 G (1 CUP) PANKO BREADCRUMBS
- 1 EGG, BEATEN WITH 2 TABLESPOONS WATER
- 4 KRAFT SINGLES

Using a rolling pin, flatten the bread slices to a 2 mm (⅛ inch) thickness.

Place the panko breadcrumbs in a shallow tray, and the beaten egg in another.

Wrap a slice of cheese around each frankfurter, then wrap a slice of bread around the cheese. Dab some water along one edge of the bread and roll the hotdog on a flat surface to seal.

Dip one of the hotdogs in the egg, then roll in the panko crumbs until fully coated. Repeat the process one more time.

Immediately lower the hotdog into the hot oil and fry for 5–7 minutes, until golden brown. Remove and place on a wire rack with paper towel underneath to catch the excess oil. One at a time, coat and cook the remaining frankfurters in the same way.

Serve hot, with ketchup and mustard.

NOTES / The batter will start to set if not used immediately. If it does, add some water and stir to make it a thick batter again. The batter needs to be thick and not too runny, otherwise the fries or bread cubes won't adhere to it.

01 / FRIED BREAD HOTDOG 02 / FRENCH FRIES HOTDOG 03 / PANKO CHEESE HOTDOG

02
03
Shake and enjoy
LOTTE
Shake and enjoy

Beef meatball skewers

Tteok galbi wanja

Once cooked in palace kitchens, only to be enjoyed by royalty, Tteok galbi wanja is now a hugely popular street food. The name means 'rice cake ribs' – the traditional dish was made by cutting and mincing beef, then moulding it into the shape of rice cakes around the rib bones. Today it's made more simply as meatballs on a bamboo skewer.

SERVES 4–6

- 800 G (1 LB 12 OZ) CHUCK STEAK OR MINCED (GROUND) BEEF
- 75 G (½ CUP) PLAIN (ALL-PURPOSE) FLOUR
- 2 TABLESPOONS OLIVE OIL
- 125 G (½ CUP) MAYONNAISE
- 1 GARLIC CLOVE, CRUSHED
- 1 TABLESPOON DILL PICKLE JUICE

MARINADE

- 60 ML (¼ CUP) SOY SAUCE
- 2 TABLESPOONS CASTER (SUPERFINE) SUGAR
- 2 TABLESPOONS MIRIN
- 3 TABLESPOONS GRATED NASHI OR ASIAN PEAR
- ½ ONION, FINELY DICED
- 2 SPRING ONIONS (SCALLIONS), THINLY SLICED
- 3 GARLIC CLOVES, FINELY CHOPPED
- 2 CM (¾ IN) PIECE OF GINGER, PEELED AND FINELY GRATED
- 1 TABLESPOON SESAME OIL
- ½ TEASPOON FRESHLY GROUND BLACK PEPPER
- 1 TABLESPOON GOCHUGARU
- 1 TABLESPOON GOCHUJANG

If you are using chuck steak, cut the meat into thin strips, then again crossways into smaller pieces. Rock the knife blade back and forth until the meat resembles a coarse paste. Skip this step if using minced beef. Transfer the beef to a large bowl.

To make the marinade, combine all the ingredients in a bowl and mix well. Pour the marinade over the beef and, using your hands, knead the beef for about 3 minutes, until well combined and sticky. Cover with plastic wrap and transfer to the fridge for at least 2 hours, or preferably overnight.

Soak 12 bamboo skewers in water for 30 minutes. Prepare a charcoal grill and wait for the coals to die down to a coating of white ash – this will take about an hour.

Meanwhile, roll a heaped tablespoon of the beef mixture into a golf ball–sized meatball. Put the flour in a bowl and dredge the meatball in flour, shaking off any excess. Transfer to a baking tray. Repeat until all the beef mixture is used. Thread three meatballs onto each bamboo skewer.

Heat the olive oil in a frying pan over medium heat. In small batches, fry the meatballs for 3–4 minutes, until thoroughly cooked and slightly charred on the outside. Transfer the meatballs to the charcoal grill and cook, turning occasionally, for 4–5 minutes.

Meanwhile, combine the mayonnaise, garlic and dill pickle juice in a small bowl and mix well.

Transfer the meatball skewers to a serving plate and drizzle with the mayonnaise. Serve immediately.

2016년 8월19일 방영 매스컴에서 소개한집
우와
떴다 야식이 먹방
위생점검 거리가게
주덮밥
536903
(장현주)
먹어본

SEVENTEEN
세븐틴 코인노래 연습장 4F
SEVENTEEN
세븐틴 코인노래 연습장 3F
5층
라운지
포켓볼
4F
펍그린
당구장
무청감자탕
감자탕
뼈구이
해장국
시래기감자탕 & 숯불뼈구이 전문점
홍대
만남의 광장
소주
맥주
안주
?
국내 최대 60개룸
단체석 많아요
0개룸
방 vs 방
통화 채팅 게임
안주 맛집 헌팅 명가
룸의 정석
신개념 룸주점
2,3F
안주 맛집
신개념 룸주점
룸의정석
헌팅 명가
룸의 정석
신개념 룸주점
2F,3F
홍대점 02-612-1114
슈퍼방구

Tornado potato hotdog sticks

Hoeoligamja

When East meets West at the street-food cart, delicious magic can happen. If you're lucky, what you get is a hotdog wrapped in a spiral cut potato, battered, then deep-fried until crunchily golden.

MAKES 4

- 2 FLOURY POTATOES, SUCH AS RUSSETS OR COLIBANS, SKIN ON
- 4 HOTDOG FRANKFURTERS
- VEGETABLE OIL, FOR FRYING
- SALT, FOR SEASONING

TEMPURA BATTER

- 1 EGG
- 250 ML (1 CUP) ICED WATER
- 150 G (1 CUP) PLAIN (ALL-PURPOSE) FLOUR, SIFTED

TO SERVE

- KETCHUP, MAYONNAISE OR MUSTARD (OR A MIX)

NOTE / It is important that the oil is hot enough to flash-fry the potato quickly. If it is not, the hotdog will start to expand and the skin will split, causing the potato spiral to fall apart.

Soak four bamboo skewers in water for 30 minutes.

To make the tempura batter, whisk the egg and water in a large bowl until combined. A little at a time, sprinkle the flour into the egg mixture, whisking constantly. Be careful not to over-whisk, as a few lumps of flour in the batter will give you nice crispy bits once fried. Pour the batter into a jug and refrigerate until ready to use.

Wash the potatoes and pat them dry with paper towel. Using a potato spiral cutter, cut the potatoes into long spirals according to the manufacturer's instructions. Using an apple corer, punch a hole through the centre of the potatoes lengthways. Then cut each potato in half to make two spirals.

Insert a bamboo skewer lengthways through each frankfurter until the tip of the skewer comes out the other end. Thread each frankfurter through the hole of a potato spiral, then gently spread out the potato layers like an accordion and wrap them around the whole sausage. Secure the potato in place by piercing the top layer of potato with the skewer.

Heat 5 cm (2 in) of vegetable oil in a large wok over medium–high heat until it reaches 190°C (375°F) on a kitchen thermometer. Give the batter a quick stir. Holding a potato skewer over a large container, pour some of the batter over the skewer until fully coated, allowing the excess to drip into the container. Carefully lower the skewer into the hot oil and deep-fry, turning occasionally, for 2 minutes or until the potato is golden and crispy. Remove and transfer to a wire rack with paper towel underneath to catch the excess oil. Repeat with the remaining skewers.

To serve, season the potato skewers with salt while they are still hot and serve immediately on their own or with your choice of sauce.

포도

Pork mandu

Gogi mandu

This classic street-food dumpling has a juicy filling of pork, glass noodles, cabbage, garlic chives and ginger. The word 'mandu' captures any kind of filled dumpling in Korea: meat or vegetable, steamed, deep-fried, pan-fried or floating in soup broth. Invite your friends over, cover the benchtop with these delicate thin wrappers and filling, and enjoy a dumpling-making party. Everyone takes a batch and goes home happy.

MAKES 32

- 200 G (7 OZ) NAPA (CHINESE) CABBAGE, FINELY CHOPPED
- 1 TEASPOON SALT
- 80 G (2¾ OZ) KOREAN GLASS NOODLES
- 300 G (10½ OZ) MINCED (GROUND) PORK, WITH 30% FAT
- 1 BUNCH OF GARLIC CHIVES, THINLY SLICED
- 3-4 SPRING ONIONS (SCALLIONS), THINLY SLICED
- 2 TABLESPOONS SOY SAUCE
- 2 TABLESPOONS MIRIN
- 1 TEASPOON MINCED GINGER WITH JUICE
- 1 TABLESPOON SESAME OIL
- 1 TEASPOON GROUND WHITE PEPPER
- VINEGAR SOY DIPPING SAUCE (PAGE 226), TO SERVE

To make the dumpling wrappers, place the flour in a large bowl and use chopsticks to stir and loosen the flour. Gradually add the hot water, mixing as you go, then add the room temperature water and stir until the mixture forms rough flour crumbs. Use your hands to knead the flour mixture into a rough dough, then cover and leave to rest for 10–15 minutes.

Transfer the dough to a clean work surface and knead it into a smooth dough. If it still feels stiff and rough, rest the dough for another 10 minutes, then knead again. Finally, rest the dough, covered, for 30–60 minutes, until soft.

Meanwhile, place the cabbage in a non-reactive bowl, sprinkle with the salt and toss together. Set aside for 30 minutes, then drain and squeeze the cabbage to remove the excess liquid.

Bring a saucepan of water to the boil over medium–high heat, add the glass noodles and cook for 5–6 minutes, until soft. Drain and rinse under cold running water, then use a pair of kitchen scissors to snip the noodles into small pieces.

Place the pork, cabbage, noodles, garlic chives and spring onion in a large bowl and use your hand to mix everything together. Add the soy sauce, mirin, ginger, sesame oil and pepper, and mix for 1–2 minutes, until everything is well incorporated. The mixture should be sticky but not wet.

DUMPLING WRAPPERS

250 G (1⅔ CUPS) PLAIN (ALL-PURPOSE) FLOUR, PLUS EXTRA FOR DUSTING

80 ML (⅓ CUP) HOT WATER

50 ML (1¾ FL OZ) ROOM TEMPERATURE WATER

Lightly flour your work surface, then roll the dough into a long log about 2.5 cm (1 in) thick. Cut the log into four even pieces, then cut each piece into eight and roll into balls – they should weigh about 10 g (⅓ oz) each. Cover the dough balls with a tea towel or transfer to a container to prevent them drying out.

Working with one ball of dough at a time, press the dough with the palm of your hand to flatten it slightly, then use a rolling pin to roll it into a thin round wrapper, 8–10 cm (3¼–4 in) wide. Repeat with the remaining dough, stacking the wrappers and gently dusting with flour to prevent them sticking.

Place a wrapper in the palm of your hand and spread a heaped tablespoon of the filling in the centre of the wrapper. Fold the wrapper in half, then pinch the centre together. On the left side, fold the two sides of the wrapper inwards and pinch to make a pleat, then repeat to make two more pleats. Repeat on the right-hand side, until the dumpling is completely sealed. Place the mandu on a tray lightly dusted with flour and repeat with the remaining dumpling wrappers and filling.

Working in batches, steam the dumplings in a large bamboo steamer for 7–8 minutes, until cooked through. Serve with the vinegar soy dipping sauce.

TRAVEL MASTER

Near inflammables
Balanced
Drip-Pan
•Container groove must be fitted as in the above figure
TM2000
Min.
OFF

Cheesy eggy bread

Gyeran ppang

This will play delicious tricks with your senses. Are you tasting a sweet muffin, or a salty–cheesy egg roll? Gyeran ppang translates as 'egg bread' and this fluffy loaf with a stick of mozzarella inside manages to be simultaneously sweet and savoury. While Gyeran ppang is usually eaten as a street-food snack, it also makes a really great breakfast – add some ham or bacon and a drizzle of maple syrup.

MAKES 6

- 50 G (1¾ OZ) BUTTER, MELTED, PLUS EXTRA FOR GREASING
- 115 G (½ CUP) CASTER (SUPERFINE) SUGAR, PLUS EXTRA FOR SPRINKLING
- 125 ML (½ CUP) FULL-CREAM (WHOLE) MILK
- ½ TEASPOON VANILLA EXTRACT
- 8 LARGE EGGS
- 150 G (1 CUP) SELF-RAISING FLOUR
- 3 MOZZARELLA STICKS, HALVED

Combine the butter, sugar, milk, vanilla extract and two of the eggs in a bowl and whisk to combine. Add the flour and whisk until you have a smooth batter with no lumps. Pour the batter into a jug and set aside.

Preheat the oven to 200°C (400°F). Brush the bottom and sides of six 9 × 5 cm (3½ × 2 in) loaf (bar) tins with butter. Half-fill each tin with batter, then place half a mozzarella stick on top and bake for 10 minutes.

Open the oven door and carefully slide the oven rack out. Crack an egg on top of each loaf, then sprinkle some sugar over the top. Slide the rack back into the oven and bake for another 10 minutes or until the eggs are just cooked and the yolks are still slightly runny.

Remove the tins from the oven and leave to rest for a couple of minutes before gently turning out the loaves. Serve warm, perhaps with a side of crispy bacon.

Crispy pancakes with brown sugar nut filling

Hotteok

Crisp on the outside and chewy on the inside, with a sweet cinnamon-flavoured brown sugar filling that is highly addictive, there is nothing to rival this traditional pancake. Piping hot, fresh from a street-food vendor, this is my idea of a perfect winter treat.

MAKES 4

- 115 G (½ CUP) LIGHT BROWN SUGAR
- ½ TEASPOON GROUND CINNAMON
- 40 G (1½ OZ) WALNUTS, TOASTED AND FINELY CHOPPED

DOUGH

- 150 ML (5 FL OZ) LUKEWARM WATER
- 1 TABLESPOON CASTER (SUPERFINE) SUGAR
- 1 TEASPOON DRIED YEAST
- 1 TABLESPOON VEGETABLE OIL, PLUS EXTRA FOR GREASING AND FRYING
- 130 G (4½ OZ) PLAIN (ALL-PURPOSE) FLOUR, PLUS EXTRA FOR DUSTING
- 80 G (2¾ OZ) GLUTINOUS RICE FLOUR
- ½ TEASPOON SALT

To make the dough, pour the water into a bowl and mix in the sugar, yeast and vegetable oil. Stir, and leave to sit for 5 minutes or until the mixture is foamy.

Sift the plain and rice flours into a large mixing bowl and stir in the salt. Add the yeast mixture and stir with a fork to form a wet dough. Scrape the dough onto a lightly floured work surface and knead for 2–3 minutes, until the dough is smooth and elastic. Place the dough back in the bowl, cover with plastic wrap, and leave to prove in a warm place for 1 hour or until the dough has doubled in size.

Meanwhile, place the brown sugar, cinnamon and walnuts in a bowl and stir to combine. Set aside until ready to use.

Turn the dough out onto a lightly floured work surface and knead for another 2 minutes. Shape the dough into a log, then divide into four equal pieces. Roll each piece into a ball.

Grease both hands with a little vegetable oil. Grab a dough ball and flatten it out by pressing it firmly between the palms of your hands until it is about 5 mm (¼ in) thick. Pinch a 1 cm (½ in) border around the edge of the dough to flatten it slightly, so that it's not too thick when you fold it over later. Repeat with the remaining balls of dough.

Put one-quarter of the nut filling in the centre of each disc of dough. Fold the edges over the filling and pinch together to seal like a parcel. Make sure the filling is completely sealed, otherwise it will leak out when frying.

Place the filled dough balls, seam side down, on a baking tray lined with baking paper. Gently flatten the balls with the palm of your hand until they are about 1 cm (½ in) thick.

Heat about 250 ml (1 cup) of vegetable oil in a large frying pan over medium heat. Oil a wide spatula by dipping it into the oil in the pan so it won't stick when flipping the pancakes.

Fry two pancakes at a time in the hot oil, seam side down, leaving some space between them so they don't stick together. Fry for 2 minutes, then carefully flip and fry for another 2 minutes on the other side. If the pancakes start to brown too quickly, reduce the heat to medium–low. Use the spatula to press the pancakes down in the oil so they cook evenly. The pancakes are ready when both sides are golden brown and crispy.

Remove the pancakes from the pan and transfer to a wire rack with paper towel underneath to catch the excess oil.

Allow the pancakes to cool for 3–5 minutes before eating as the filling will be very hot.

NOTE / The hotteok can be stored at room temperature for 1-2 days or in the fridge for 1 week. When you're ready to serve, fry the pancakes in a lightly oiled frying pan over medium heat until warmed through and crispy on both sides. Alternatively, you can warm them in a preheated 200°C (400°F) oven for 10 minutes, or in the microwave.

DREAM OF TEA
Lemon

Korean shaved ice

Pat bingsu

The best way to combat sweltering summer heat is undoubtedly a glorious mountain of pat bingsu – a vibrant heap of ice shavings adorned with sweet red bean paste, chewy rice cake and an array of fruits. It's a kaleidoscope of flavours and colours. Kids love it; adults too. You'll need an ice shaver here – they're widely available and inexpensive, and, when you've made pat bingsu once, you'll find yourself making it on every hot day. So, it's an investment!

SERVES 1

- 400 G (2 CUPS) SHAVED ICE (SEE NOTE)
- 100 G (½ CUP) TINNED SWEET RED (ANKO) BEANS
- 2 STRAWBERRIES, HULLED AND CUT INTO SMALL PIECES
- 1 KIWI FRUIT, PEELED AND CUT INTO SMALL PIECES
- 50 G (1¾ OZ) STICKY RICE DOUGH (PAGE 66), CUT INTO SMALL CUBES
- 2 SCOOPS OF VANILLA ICE CREAM
- 2 TABLESPOONS SWEETENED CONDENSED MILK (OPTIONAL)

Pile the shaved ice in a shallow serving bowl. Scatter over the red beans, strawberry, kiwi fruit and cubes of sticky rice dough. Top with the ice cream and drizzle with sweetened condensed milk, if desired.

To eat, mix a little bit of everything with the shaved ice to form a flavoured icy drink and slurp it up! Serve immediately.

NOTE / An ice shaver can be found at any department store or online. Unfortunately, food processors and blenders tend to crush the ice rather than shaving it into the thin shards required for this dessert.

고추방앗간
청주상회
02-853-3293
구로시장
청주상회

노각
2,000
여주
1,000
1949
금남시장
5번길
맛집
금호
모텔
김경자원조손칼국수
겉절이 · 각종김치
각종전 (주문받습니다)
원조반찬
칼국수 · 보쌈
원조
금호동 맛집
보 쌈
손칼국수
칼 제 비
떡 만 두
떡 국
금호식당

Goldfish bread

Bungeoppang

This traditional goldfish-shaped pastry is the perfect winter hand-warmer – especially when it arrives hot and crispy, straight from the pan. Bite into the waffle coating and you'll find a gooey surprise filling of sweet red bean paste. It's no wonder this has been the most popular sweet street snack in Korea since the 1950s. Nowadays, you'll find bungeoppang filled with custard, chocolate and even pizza toppings.

MAKES 6

- 100 G (⅔ CUP) PLAIN (ALL-PURPOSE) FLOUR
- 45 G (¼ CUP) RICE FLOUR
- ½ TEASPOON SALT
- ½ TEASPOON BAKING SODA
- ½ TEASPOON BAKING POWDER
- 2 TABLESPOONS CASTER (SUPERFINE) SUGAR
- 1 EGG
- 185 ML (¾ CUP) FULL-CREAM (WHOLE) MILK
- VEGETABLE OIL, FOR BRUSHING
- 3 TABLESPOONS SWEET RED (ANKO) BEAN PASTE

EQUIPMENT

- 1 × GOLDFISH BAKING MOULD

Sift all the dry ingredients into a large bowl. In another bowl, whisk the egg and milk together. Pour the egg mixture into the dry ingredients and whisk until you have a smooth batter with no lumps. Pour the batter through a fine-mesh sieve into a jug.

The goldfish mould can make two bread fish at a time. Heat the mould in a frying pan for 2 minutes over medium heat until it is nice and hot, then reduce the heat to low. Carefully open the mould and brush the inside lightly with vegetable oil.

Pour some batter into the fish shapes until they are about one-third full; just enough to cover the bottom. Add 2 teaspoons of red bean paste to the centre of each fish, making sure not to overfill them or the batter will spill out when cooking and won't seal properly. Pour in enough of the remaining batter to cover the red bean paste and fill the fish shapes.

Seal the mould tightly and cook for 3–4 minutes over medium heat, then turn the mould over and cook for another 3 minutes on the other side. Open the mould to check the bread is cooked. It should be golden and crispy on both sides. If it's not, reseal the mould and cook for another 1–2 minutes, turning regularly, until the bread is cooked. Remove from the heat.

Carefully remove the bread fish from the mould and serve while they are still piping hot. Repeat with the remaining batter and bean paste to make six in all.

Sticky rice dumplings

Chapssaltteok

Chapssaltteok is a popular Korean treat akin to Japanese mochi cakes. These sweet and chewy glutinous rice dumplings, filled with red bean paste, are typically served as a sweet bite with tea when guests drop by. They also symbolise good luck, and a batch of them makes a perfect little gift for friends and family.

MAKES 8

200 G (7 OZ) TINNED SWEET RED (ANKO) BEANS

STICKY RICE DOUGH

175 G (1 CUP) GLUTINOUS RICE FLOUR

55 G (¼ CUP) CASTER (SUPERFINE) SUGAR

PINCH OF SALT

CORNFLOUR (CORNSTARCH), FOR DUSTING

Put the red beans in a food processor or use a hand-held blender to blend the beans to a fine paste. The paste should be thick, but not wet. Take 2 tablespoons of the paste and roll it into a ball with your hands. Repeat with the remaining paste to make eight balls. Transfer them to a baking tray lined with baking paper and set aside until ready to use.

To make the sticky rice dough, combine the rice flour, sugar and salt in a heatproof bowl and stir to combine. Stirring continuously, gradually add 250 ml (1 cup) of water in a steady stream. Stir until a thick paste forms. Cover the bowl with plastic wrap and transfer to the microwave. Cook the mixture on high for 3 minutes, then carefully remove the bowl (it will be hot) and beat the mixture vigorously with a wooden spoon. The dough should be stretchy and translucent. If it is not, microwave for another 30 seconds and beat again. Continue until you achieve the right consistency, then set aside to cool slightly.

Once the dough is cool enough to handle, turn it out onto a work surface dusted liberally with cornflour. Sprinkle a little extra cornflour over the top of the dough to prevent it from sticking, then roll the dough out to a 5 mm (¼ in) thickness. Dip the blade of a sharp knife or pizza cutter in some cornflour, then cut out eight even-sized circles about 10 cm (4 in) in diameter.

Take one disc of dough and use a pastry brush to gently dust off any excess cornflour. Place a ball of red bean filling in the centre of the disc, then fold the edges over the filling and pinch together to seal. Gently roll it in your hands to form a smooth ball, then place it, seam side down, on a baking tray dusted with cornflour. Repeat with the remaining dough and filling to make eight dumplings.

Store the dumplings in an airtight container at room temperature and eat within 1–2 days.

Honeycomb candy

Ppopgi

Ppopgi are popular street snacks for children in Korea, not only because they're tasty, but they're also fun to eat! *Squid Game* viewers now know that Ppopgi are made with a shape stamped in the middle – the goal is to nibble around the outline, or scratch out the shape with a needle, without the honeycomb cracking. If you succeed, you can treat yourself to another (or live to compete another day). Fun for your next dinner party with friends!

MAKES 4

- BUTTER, FOR GREASING
- 115 G (½ CUP) CASTER (SUPERFINE) SUGAR
- ½ TEASPOON BAKING SODA

NOTE / Get creative with this recipe by sprinkling some granulated sugar, toasted sesame seeds or finely crushed nuts onto the baking sheet before pouring on the honeycomb. You can also pour the honeycomb over bamboo skewers to make lollipops!

First, set up a stamping station. Cut two sheets of baking paper the same size as a large baking sheet. Use one piece of paper to line the baking sheet and grease the paper well with butter. Grease one side of the other piece of baking paper with butter and set aside. Find a heavy object with a flat surface, such as a wooden chopping board or a couple of heavy cookbooks. You will also need a few cookie cutters in different shapes, ready for stamping.

To make the honeycomb, heat the sugar in a small saucepan over medium heat until it begins to melt. Swirl the pan around so the sugar melts evenly and doesn't brown too quickly.

Once the sugar has melted and turned a light golden colour, remove it from the heat. Add the baking soda and beat vigorously with a wooden spoon until it stops foaming and bubbling. The honeycomb should be a light amber colour.

Immediately pour the honeycomb onto the prepared baking sheet in four equal circles about 5 cm (2 in) in diameter. Leave at least 5 cm (2 in) of space between each circle to allow for spreading. Place the second sheet of baking paper, greased side down, over the honeycomb, then place a chopping board on top for 5 seconds to weigh down the mixture. Remove the board and the top sheet of baking paper, then use various cookie cutters to stamp different shapes into the honeycomb, being careful not to cut all the way through. Work quickly, while the honeycomb is still malleable.

Set aside to cool and harden, then eat the honeycomb immediately or store it in an airtight container. Be sure to layer the honeycomb with baking paper to prevent them sticking together.

Anju
Anju

안주안주

THE NEXT TIME YOU INVITE FRIENDS OVER, DITCH THE CHIPS AND DIPS AND FOLLOW A FOOD TRADITION THAT'S BEEN PERFECTED OVER A THOUSAND YEARS. ANJU ARE THE IRRESISTIBLE, MOUTH-WATERING, MEATY, CHEESY, SALTY, SPICY (OFTEN SUPER- SPICY!), DEEP-FRIED CRUNCHY SNACKS THAT ARE ENJOYED WITH DRINKS IN UBER-COOL SEOUL BARS AND TRADITIONAL COUNTRY TAVERNS ALIKE.

MUCH LIKE STREET FOOD, THE ANJU SCENE IS CONSTANTLY ON THE MOVE. THE MOST POPULAR AND FAMOUS NIBBLES ARE JEON – CRISP-BATTERED, SOFT-CENTRED PANCAKES THAT CAN BE MADE FROM VEGETABLES, MINCED FISH OR MEAT, AND EVEN KIMCHI. IN RECENT YEARS THE TRADITIONAL SPICY STIR-FRIES AND FRITTERS HAVE BEEN JOINED BY MODERN FUSION VARIATIONS – ALL ARE DESIGNED TO BOTH COMPLEMENT THE FLAVOUR OF THE DRINKS AND PROLONG THE FUN OF THE GATHERING BY SOAKING UP THE ALCOHOL, WHICH SOUNDS LIKE THE PERFECT BRIEF FOR A BAR SNACK!

SO, NOW WHEN YOU'RE ENTERTAINING, BRING OUT A TRAY OF CHEESY FIRE CHICKEN OR CRISP-JUICY KFC. JUST MAKE SURE YOU HAVE PLENTY OF COLD BEER ON HAND TO WASH THEM DOWN.

Fritters

Jeon

On birthdays, festive holidays and even for dinner parties, the Korean way to celebrate is often by cooking up a feast of jeon – crisp-battered finger-food fritters with a variety of fillings. Set up the kitchen with chopping, dusting, frying and dipping sauce stations, give everyone a job and get these hot, crunchy fritters rolling out!

SERVES 8–10

150 G (1 CUP) PLAIN (ALL-PURPOSE) FLOUR

3 EGGS, LIGHTLY BEATEN

VEGETABLE OIL, FOR SHALLOW-FRYING

SPICY SOY AND SPRING ONION SAUCE (PAGE 223), TO SERVE

ZUCCHINI FRITTERS

2 ZUCCHINI (COURGETTES)

1 TEASPOON SALT

FISH FRITTERS

250 G (9 OZ) SKINLESS COD FISH FILLETS, OR OTHER FIRM WHITE-FLESHED FISH, SUCH AS LING, SOLE OR HADDOCK

SALT AND FRESHLY GROUND BLACK PEPPER, TO TASTE

To make the zucchini fritters, cut the zucchini into 5 mm (¼ in) thick rounds. Place them in a bowl, sprinkle with the salt and toss well. Spread them out in a single layer on a baking tray and set aside for 10 minutes to draw out some of the moisture. Rinse, and spread them out on paper towels to dry. Set aside, ready for frying.

For the fish fritters, lay the fillets flat on a chopping board. Starting from one end, slice the fillets on an angle into 1 cm (½ in) thick slices. Transfer to a baking tray, season with salt and pepper on both sides, and set aside, ready for frying.

To make the beef fritters, combine all the ingredients in a large bowl and mix well until the mixture is sticky and pasty, about 2–3 minutes. Set aside half of the mixture for the green chilli fritters.

Roll a heaped tablespoon of the remaining beef mixture into a ball, then press it down to make a small patty. Transfer to a baking tray lined with baking paper, then repeat with the remaining mince. Set aside, ready for frying.

For the stuffed chilli fritters, trim the stems from the chillies and cut them in half lengthways. Discard the seeds and membranes. Stuff each chilli half with 2 teaspoons of the reserved beef mixture. Transfer them to a baking tray lined with baking paper, ready for frying.

Set up a dusting station. Place the flour in a shallow bowl, and put the beaten egg in another shallow bowl. Heat 2 tablespoons vegetable oil in a frying pan over medium–high heat.

BEEF FRITTERS

- 500 G (1 LB 2 OZ) MINCED (GROUND) BEEF
- ½ CARROT, FINELY CHOPPED
- ½ ONION, FINELY CHOPPED
- 1 SPRING ONION (SCALLION), THINLY SLICED
- 2 GARLIC CLOVES, CRUSHED
- 2 CM (¾ IN) PIECE OF GINGER, PEELED AND FINELY GRATED
- 1 TEASPOON SALT
- ½ TEASPOON FRESHLY GROUND BLACK PEPPER
- 1 TEASPOON SESAME OIL
- 1 EGG, LIGHTLY BEATEN

STUFFED CHILLI FRITTERS

- 10 LARGE GREEN CHILLIES
- 250 G (9 OZ) OF THE BEEF FRITTER MIXTURE ABOVE

Start with the zucchini. Working with a few slices at a time, dredge the zucchini in the flour, dusting off any excess, then dip in the beaten egg and transfer to the frying pan. Cook for 2 minutes on each side or until golden brown. Transfer to a wire rack with paper towels underneath to catch the excess oil.

Working in small batches, dredge the fish pieces in the flour, dusting off any excess, then dip in the beaten egg. If the frying pan seems dry, add another tablespoon of oil. Fry the fish for 2–3 minutes on each side, until golden brown. Remove to the wire rack and leave to drain.

Repeat the process with the beef patties, frying for 2–3 minutes on each side, and the stuffed chillies. Serve immediately or at room temperature with the spicy soy and spring onion sauce for dipping.

01 / FISH FRITTERS 02 / ZUCCHINI FRITTERS 03 / STUFFED CHILLI FRITTERS 04 / BEEF FRITTERS

04

Spring onion pancake

Pajeon

Pajeon is one of the most popular and traditional Korean pancakes. It's easy to see why these are so beloved – it only takes a few minutes to whip up a batch, which is always satisfyingly impressive if friends drop by unexpectedly! Young, skinny, green spring onions are best for this recipe: the older, fatter ones can be a bit tough.

MAKES 2

1 × QUANTITY KOREAN PANCAKE MIX (PAGE 231)

4 SPRING ONIONS (SCALLIONS)

VEGETABLE OIL, FOR FRYING

Prepare the pancake mix, following the recipe on page 231, then set aside.

Trim the roots off the spring onions and cut into 8–10 cm (3¼–4 in) lengths. If the white parts are thick, split them in half lengthways.

Heat 2 tablespoons vegetable oil in a 20 cm (8 in) non-stick frying pan over medium heat. Give the batter a quick stir then ladle half of the batter into the pan. Use the back of the ladle to spread the batter out to the edge of the pan. Lay half the spring onion in a single layer on top of the batter. Fry the pancake for 4–5 minutes, until golden brown on the bottom. Use a wide spatula to flip the pancake over. Cook for a further 4–5 minutes, until golden brown.

Transfer the pancake to a baking tray lined with paper towel to soak up any excess oil. Repeat with the remaining batter and spring onion.

Cut the pancakes into large squares and serve warm.

NOTE / You can also make garlic chive pancakes by substituting the spring onions for 50 g (1¾ oz) garlic chives. They are just as good.

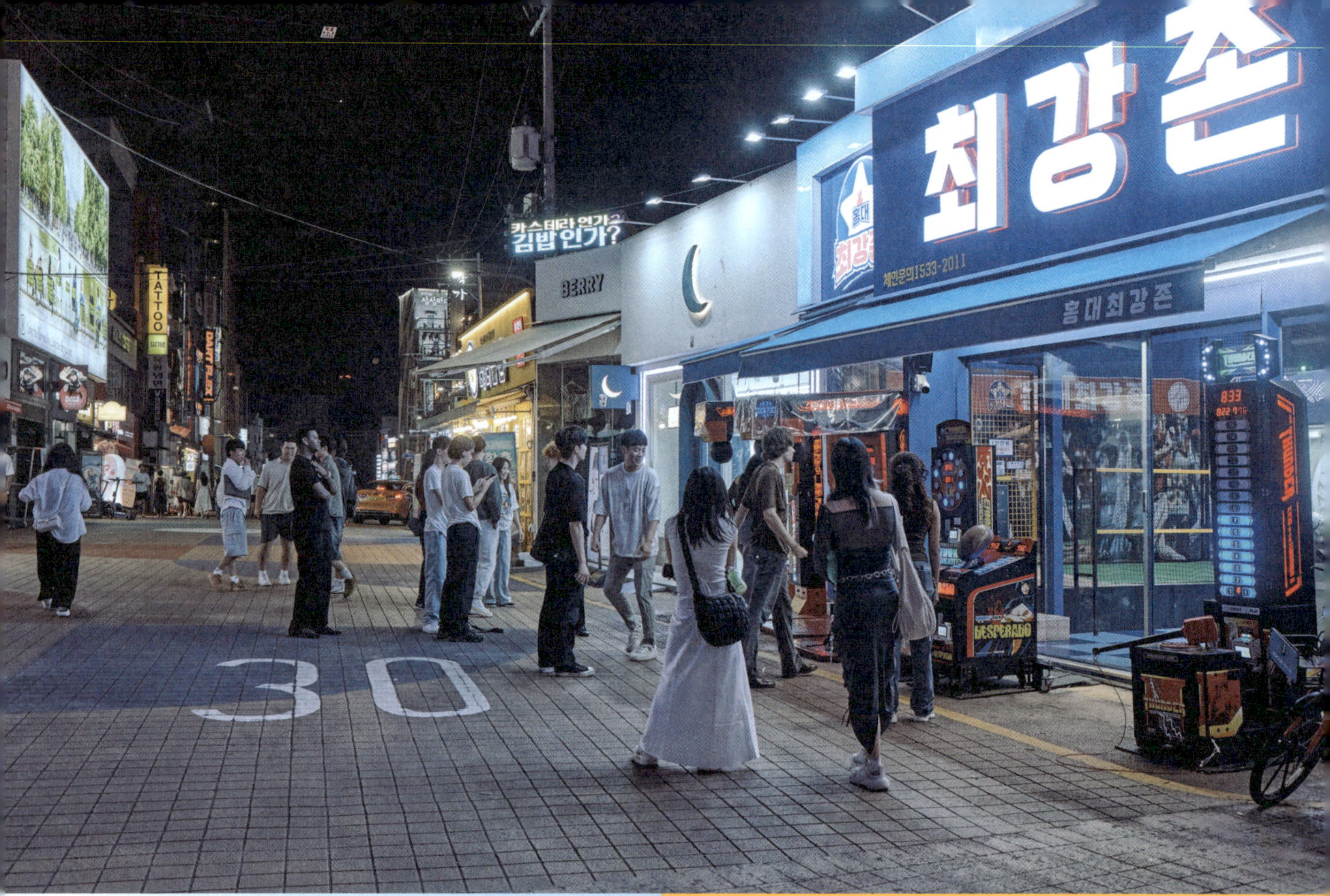
카스테라 인가?
김밥 인가?
BERRY
TATTOO
최강존
체인문의1533-2011
홍대최강존
30
DESPERADO

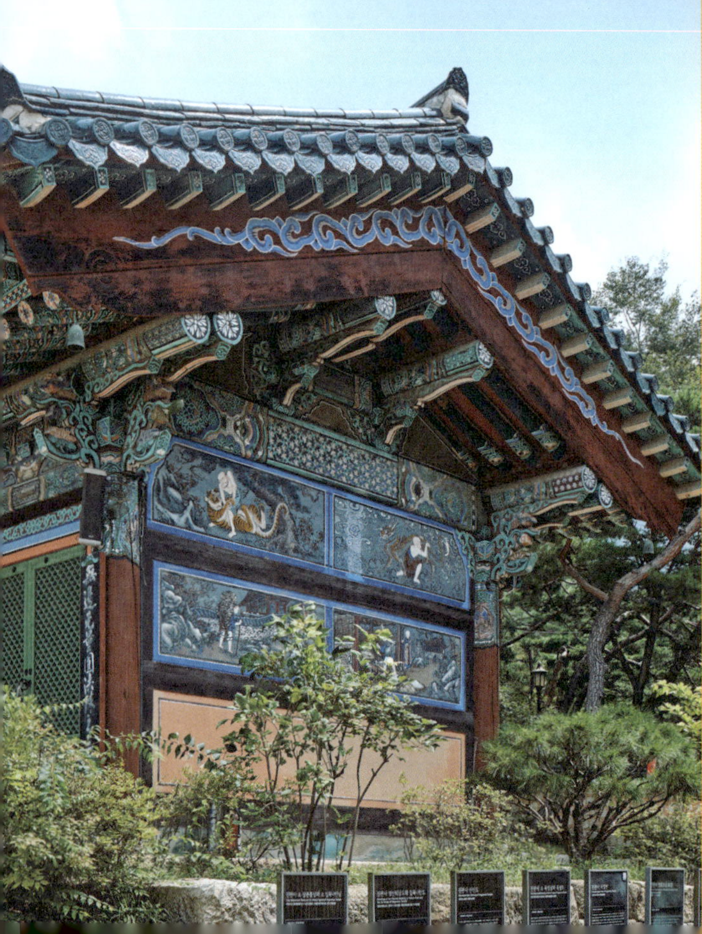

Seafood spring onion pancakes

Haemul pajeon

Once you've mastered the basic Pajeon (page 78), it's time to get a little fancy and bring some seafood to the party. This is always one of the most popular orders at any Korean restaurant – and you can't argue with popularity! The crispy pancake batter studded with mixed seafood creates an intriguingly delicious range of textures and flavours.

MAKES 2

- 1 × QUANTITY KOREAN PANCAKE MIX (PAGE 231)
- 4 SPRING ONIONS (SCALLIONS), PLUS EXTRA, SLICED, TO SERVE
- VEGETABLE OIL, FOR FRYING
- 200 G (1 CUP) MIXED SEAFOOD, SUCH AS CALAMARI, SALMON AND PEELED PRAWNS (SHRIMP)
- 1 EGG, LIGHTLY BEATEN
- SPICY SOY AND SPRING ONION SAUCE (PAGE 223), TO SERVE

Prepare the pancake mix, following the recipe on page 231, then set aside.

Trim the roots off the spring onions, then cut into 5 cm (2 in) lengths. If the white parts are thick, split them in half lengthways.

Heat 2 tablespoons vegetable oil in a 20 cm (8 in) non-stick frying pan over medium heat. Add half the seafood and fry for 2 minutes, until slightly browned. Spoon half of the beaten egg over the seafood.

Give the batter a quick stir then ladle half of the batter into the pan. Use the back of the ladle to spread the batter out to the edge of the pan. Lay half the spring onion in a single layer on top of the batter. Fry the pancake for 4–5 minutes, until golden brown on the bottom. Use a wide spatula to flip the pancake over. Add another tablespoon of oil, press the pancake down with the back of the spatula, and cook for a further 4–5 minutes, until golden brown.

Transfer the pancake to a baking tray lined with paper towel to soak up any excess oil. Repeat with the remaining batter and ingredients.

Serve the pancakes immediately, with extra spring onion scattered over the top, and the soy and spring onion dipping sauce on the side.

Kimchi pancakes with pork belly

Kimchi jeon

If you've had a jar of kimchi fermenting in the fridge for weeks, the time has come to chop some up and make kimchi jeon. This spicy pancake is the perfect comfort food for any cold rainy evening. (Or warm sunny lunchtime with a cold drink!) You could make a simpler version with just kimchi, but I love the extra excitement of the crispy pork belly here.

SERVES 4

- 1 × QUANTITY KOREAN PANCAKE MIX (PAGE 231)
- 60 ML (¼ CUP) KIMCHI JUICE
- 150 G (1 CUP) CABBAGE KIMCHI (PAGE 16), THINLY SLICED
- VEGETABLE OIL, FOR FRYING
- 100 G (3½ OZ) PORK BELLY, THINLY SLICED
- 1 SPRING ONION (SCALLION), THINLY SLICED

Prepare the pancake mix, adding the kimchi juice and enough water to make a smooth, pourable batter. Add the sliced kimchi, reserving some to garnish. Stir to combine and set aside.

Heat 2 tablespoons vegetable oil in a 20 cm (8 in) non-stick frying pan over medium heat. Fry half of the pork belly slices for 2–3 minutes, until lightly browned. Give the batter a quick stir, then ladle half of the batter over the pork belly. Use the back of the ladle to spread the batter out to the edge of the pan. Fry the pancake for 4–5 minutes, until browned on the bottom. Use a wide spatula to flip the pancake over. Add another tablespoon of oil, press the pancake down with the back of the spatula and cook for a further 4–5 minutes, until browned and the pork belly is cooked through.

Transfer the pancake to a baking tray lined with paper towel to soak up any excess oil. Repeat with the remaining batter and ingredients.

To serve, garnish both pancakes with the spring onion and reserved kimchi.

Cheesy fire chicken

Chijeu buldak

I read somewhere that spicy food can act as a stress relief, and this dish will certainly help distract the hectic mind. Buldak means 'fire chicken' and that is no exaggeration – this is super, super hot! In recent years, some genius decided to tone down the spiciness by covering the chicken with soothing cheese and, since then, the popularity of this cheesy, spicy chicken has sky-rocketed worldwide. Consider yourself warned: it is definitely not for the faint-hearted!

SERVES 4–6

- 1 KG (2 LB 3 OZ) SKINLESS CHICKEN THIGH FILLETS, TRIMMED AND CUT INTO BITE-SIZED PIECES
- 2 TABLESPOONS VEGETABLE OIL
- 250 G (1⅔ CUPS) SHREDDED MOZZARELLA
- 1 SPRING ONION (SCALLION), THINLY SLICED
- 2 HEADS COS (ROMAINE) OR BUTTER (BIBB) LETTUCE

FIRE CHICKEN MARINADE

- 65 G (½ CUP) GOCHUGARU
- 70 G (¼ CUP) GOCHUJANG
- 2 TABLESPOONS KOREAN RICE SYRUP (SSALYEOT) OR CORN SYRUP, GLUCOSE OR HONEY
- 1 TABLESPOON CASTER (SUPERFINE) SUGAR
- 2 TABLESPOONS SOY SAUCE
- 1 TABLESPOON SESAME OIL
- ½ TEASPOON FRESHLY GROUND BLACK PEPPER
- 5 GARLIC CLOVES, FINELY CHOPPED
- 5 CM (2 IN) PIECE OF GINGER, PEELED AND FINELY GRATED

To make the fire chicken marinade, combine all the ingredients in a bowl and mix well. Add the chicken to the marinade and mix until the meat is completely coated. Cover, and leave to marinate in the fridge for at least 1 hour.

Heat the vegetable oil in a large non-stick frying pan or wok over high heat. Add the chicken and stir-fry for 5 minutes. Add 60 ml (¼ cup) of water, then reduce the heat to medium and simmer, covered, for another 5 minutes. Remove the lid and increase the heat to medium–high. Cook, stirring constantly, until the sauce has reduced and thickened, about 2–3 minutes.

Preheat a grill (broiler) to high.

Sprinkle half the mozzarella over the base of a cast-iron frying pan, then arrange the chicken on top. Scatter with the remaining mozzarella, then grill for 5 minutes or until the cheese begins to brown and blister.

Scatter the spring onion over the cheesy fire chicken and serve in the pan. To eat, tear the lettuce into individual leaves and use them to wrap up the chicken like san choy bau.

cass

KFC 4 ways

Huraideu chikin

I love Korean fried chicken so much I could write a whole book about it! When I first discovered KFC, it was a revelation: the crunchy coating; the thin and crispy skin; and the super-juicy and tender meat. Colonel Sanders and his 11 secret herbs and spices just cannot compete!

Take your KFC to a whole new level with one of these amazing coatings. And crispy chicken with cheese powder? Trust me!

SERVES 4

- 1.5 KG (3 LB 5 OZ) CHICKEN WINGS, WASHED AND PATTED DRY
- ½ TEASPOON SALT, PLUS EXTRA FOR SEASONING
- ½ TEASPOON FRESHLY GROUND BLACK PEPPER
- 1 CM (½ IN) PIECE OF GINGER, PEELED AND FINELY CHOPPED
- 180 G (1 CUP) POTATO STARCH
- VEGETABLE OIL, FOR FRYING

SWEET AND SPICY

- 1 TABLESPOON VEGETABLE OIL
- 4 GARLIC CLOVES, FINELY CHOPPED
- 2 TABLESPOONS SOY SAUCE
- 2 TABLESPOONS GOCHUJANG
- 1 TABLESPOON WHITE VINEGAR
- 1 TABLESPOON KOREAN RICE SYRUP (SSALYEOT) OR CORN SYRUP, GLUCOSE OR HONEY
- 2 TABLESPOONS CASTER (SUPERFINE) SUGAR
- TOASTED SESAME SEEDS, TO SERVE

Cut the chicken wings into three parts: the meaty drumette, the wingette and the tip. Discard the tips or reserve them for another recipe. Put the chicken in a large bowl, add the salt, pepper and ginger and mix everything together well using your hands.

Put the potato starch in another bowl and dredge the chicken pieces firmly in the starch until completely coated. Shake off any excess. If there is any starch left, dredge the chicken again until all the starch has been used. Set aside for 10 minutes.

Heat about 5 cm (2 in) vegetable oil in a large heavy-based saucepan until it reaches 165°C (330°F) when tested with a kitchen thermometer. Working in batches, fry the chicken for 10–12 minutes, until light golden brown. Use tongs to turn the wings over occasionally to stop them sticking together. Remove the chicken from the oil and transfer to a wire rack with paper towel underneath to catch the excess oil.

Bring the oil temperature back to 165°C (330°F). Working in batches, fry the chicken a second time until it is deep golden brown and super crunchy, about 12–15 minutes. Remove and transfer to a wire rack with paper towel underneath to catch the excess oil.

Season the fried chicken generously with salt and serve immediately or try one of these variations.

SNOW CHEESE

- 20 G (¼ CUP) KOREAN CHEESE POWDER OR CHEDDAR CHEESE POWDER, PLUS EXTRA TO SERVE (SEE NOTE)

WASABI AND SPRING ONION

- 60 ML (¼ CUP) SOY SAUCE
- 55 G (¼ CUP) CASTER (SUPERFINE) SUGAR
- 2 TABLESPOONS MIRIN
- 1 GARLIC CLOVE, FINELY CHOPPED
- 1 TABLESPOON KOREAN RICE SYRUP (SSALYEOT) OR CORN SYRUP, GLUCOSE OR HONEY
- ½ TEASPOON SESAME OIL
- 2 TEASPOONS WASABI PASTE
- 2 SPRING ONIONS (SCALLIONS), THINLY SLICED

For the sweet and spicy sauce, heat the oil in a large non-stick frying pan or wok over medium–high heat. Add the garlic and stir-fry for 1 minute or until fragrant. Add the soy sauce, gochujang, vinegar, rice syrup and sugar, and stir until the sugar has dissolved. Reduce the heat to medium and simmer for 2–3 minutes, until the sauce has thickened and reduced by half.

Add the fried chicken to the wok and give it a quick stir to coat it in the sauce. Transfer to a serving plate, garnish with sesame seeds, and serve immediately. Alternatively, serve the fried chicken on its own with the sweet and spicy sauce on the side for dipping.

For the snow cheese variation, transfer the fried chicken to a large mixing bowl. Sprinkle over the cheese powder and toss the bowl a few times until the chicken is well coated. Transfer to a large serving plate, sprinkle with extra cheese powder, and serve immediately.

If you are making the wasabi and spring onion version, make the glaze while the chicken is cooking. Combine the soy sauce, sugar, mirin, garlic and rice syrup in a saucepan and bring to the boil over medium–high heat. Reduce the heat to medium and simmer for 2–3 minutes, until the sauce has thickened. Remove from the heat, add the sesame oil and wasabi paste and whisk until combined.

Place the fried chicken in a large mixing bowl and pour over 60 ml (¼ cup) of the wasabi glaze. Toss the bowl a few times until the chicken is well coated, adding a little more glaze if necessary. Transfer to a large serving plate and garnish with the spring onion. Serve immediately.

NOTE / 'Snow cheese' is a Korean cheddar cheese seasoning commonly used for fried chicken and noodle dishes. You can find it at Korean grocery stores or online.

01 / SWEET AND SPICY KFC 02 / WASABI AND SPRING ONION KFC 03 / SNOW CHEESE KFC 04 / ORIGINAL KFC

03
04
COLD BREWED
LAGER

ALL MALT FRESH LAGER

Corn cheese

Konchijeu

This is the must-order every time I go to a Korean barbecue restaurant. Although it's also served as a side dish, it's most popular as a bar snack. Make a batch to serve with drinks next time you're entertaining ... Sweetcorn kernels, covered in stretchy cheese and washed down with something cold. What's not to love?

SERVES 4

- 20 G (¾ OZ) UNSALTED BUTTER
- 1 × 420 G (15 OZ) TIN SWEETCORN KERNELS, DRAINED AND RINSED
- 2 SPRING ONIONS (SCALLIONS), THINLY SLICED
- 1 TABLESPOON MAYONNAISE
- 2 TEASPOONS CASTER (SUPERFINE) SUGAR
- SALT AND FRESHLY GROUND BLACK PEPPER, TO TASTE
- 100 G (⅔ CUP) SHREDDED MOZZARELLA
- CAYENNE PEPPER, FOR SPRINKLING (OPTIONAL)

Preheat a grill (broiler) to medium.

Melt the butter in a small cast-iron or ovenproof frying pan over medium heat. Add the sweetcorn kernels and fry for 3 minutes. Stir through the spring onion, then remove from the heat.

Add the mayonnaise and sugar, and season to taste with salt and pepper. Mix well, then sprinkle the cheese over the corn.

Transfer the pan to the grill for 5–8 minutes, until the cheese has melted and turned golden brown in places.

Remove from the grill and sprinkle with a little cayenne pepper, if desired. Rest for 5 minutes and serve hot, with a cold beer.

Spicy garlic-fried chicken

Kkanpunggi

Inspired by Chinese Kung Pao chicken, this fusion snack is deliciously, dangerously addictive. The crunchy, golden nuggets of chicken are coated in a spicy sweet-and-sour glaze, then tossed with crispy leek and toasted peanuts. I know the recipe says serves four, but I've occasionally smashed the whole lot on my own – I told you, it's addictive!

SERVES 4

- 500 G (1 LB 2 OZ) SKINLESS CHICKEN THIGH FILLETS
- 3 CM (1¼ IN) PIECE OF GINGER, PEELED AND FINELY GRATED
- 60 ML (¼ CUP) SOY SAUCE
- 2 TABLESPOONS MIRIN
- ½ TEASPOON BLACK PEPPER
- 180 G (1 CUP) POTATO STARCH
- 1 EGG, BEATEN
- VEGETABLE OIL, FOR FRYING
- 1 TABLESPOON CORNFLOUR (CORNSTARCH)
- ½ ONION, FINELY DICED
- 5 DRIED RED CHILLIES, CUT INTO 2 CM (¾ IN) PIECES
- 1 SPRING ONION (SCALLION), THINLY SLICED
- 2 TABLESPOONS CASTER (SUPERFINE) SUGAR
- 1 TABLESPOON WHITE VINEGAR
- 50 G (⅓ CUP) TOASTED PEANUTS

CHILLI OIL

- 60 ML (¼ CUP) VEGETABLE OIL
- 5 GARLIC CLOVES, HALVED
- 2 CM (¾ IN) PIECE OF GINGER, PEELED AND THINLY SLICED
- 1 LEEK, WHITE PART ONLY, CUT INTO THIN STRIPS
- 1 TABLESPOON GOCHUGARU

Trim the chicken thighs and cut into bite-sized pieces, then combine with the ginger, 2 tablespoons of the soy sauce, the mirin and pepper in a large bowl. Mix well, then leave to marinate in the fridge for 1 hour.

To make the chilli oil, heat the vegetable oil in a frying pan over medium heat. Add the garlic and ginger and stir-fry for 2 minutes or until the garlic is slightly charred. Add the leek and fry for another 3 minutes or until the leek has turned golden and crispy. Using a pair of tongs, remove the garlic, ginger and leek from the hot oil and reserve. Now add the gochugaru to the hot oil and cook for 1 minute, then turn off the heat and leave the oil to infuse for a few minutes. Strain the oil through a fine-mesh sieve into a heatproof bowl and set aside. Discard the gochugaru.

Add the potato starch and egg to the chicken and use your hands to massage the meat until it is well coated.

Heat 2.5 cm (1 in) vegetable oil in a wok over medium–high heat until it reaches 175°C (345°F) on a kitchen thermometer. Working in batches, fry the chicken, turning occasionally, for about 5 minutes, until golden brown and crunchy. Remove and transfer to a wire rack with paper towel underneath to catch the excess oil.

Combine the cornflour with 60 ml (¼ cup) of water and stir until smooth.

Pour the oil out of the wok and wipe it clean with paper towel. Heat the chilli oil in the same wok over medium–high heat. Add the onion and stir-fry for 2 minutes, then add the dried chilli and spring onion and cook for another minute. Add the remaining soy sauce, the sugar and white vinegar, and stir until the sugar has dissolved. Pour the cornflour mixture into the sauce and stir until smooth and thickened.

Add the chicken, fried garlic, ginger and leek to the wok, and stir in the peanuts. Mix until the chicken is nicely coated in the sauce, then transfer to a serving plate and serve immediately with steamed rice and a cold beer.

DRAFT

Stir-fried spicy pork

Jeyuk bokkeum

Loved by young and old, this is super easy to prepare and cook – and also super versatile. The juicy marinated slices of pork shoulder are wok-fried until caramelised and crispy – perfect as a speedy, crowd-pleasing bar snack, but also making a great dinner for one. Serve with crisp lettuce leaves, perilla and Spicy dipping sauce (page 222), so the pork can be wrapped and enjoyed like san choy bau, or with a big bowl of steamed rice and a few banchan as a meal.

Go ahead and cook extra to pop in the fridge for the next day; this reheats like a dream.

SERVES 4–6

- 1 KG (2 LB 3 OZ) PORK SHOULDER
- 1 ONION, THINLY SLICED
- 3 SPRING ONIONS (SCALLIONS), CUT INTO 5 CM (2 IN) LENGTHS, PLUS EXTRA, THINLY SLICED, TO SERVE
- VEGETABLE OIL, FOR FRYING

SPICY PORK MARINADE

- 135 G (½ CUP) GOCHUJANG
- 1 TABLESPOON GOCHUGARU
- 60 ML (¼ CUP) SOY SAUCE
- 2 TABLESPOONS RICE (OR WHITE) VINEGAR
- 2 TABLESPOONS CASTER (SUPERFINE) SUGAR
- 1 TABLESPOON KOREAN RICE SYRUP (SSALYEOT) OR CORN SYRUP, GLUCOSE OR HONEY
- 2 TABLESPOONS SESAME OIL
- 5 GARLIC CLOVES, FINELY CHOPPED
- 5 CM (2 IN) PIECE OF GINGER, PEELED AND FINELY GRATED

Put the pork in the freezer for about 1 hour to allow it to partially freeze and firm up, then slice the pork against the grain into 3 mm (⅛ in) thick slices. Combine the sliced pork, onion and spring onion in a large bowl and set aside.

To make the spicy pork marinade, combine all the ingredients in a bowl and stir until the sugar has dissolved. Pour the marinade over the pork and, using your hands (wear food preparation gloves if necessary), rub the marinade into the meat until it is well coated. Cover with plastic wrap and leave to marinate in the fridge for at least 1 hour.

Heat 2 tablespoons vegetable oil in a large frying pan or wok over high heat. Stir-fry the pork, in batches, for 3–4 minutes, until well browned and caramelised. Add a little more oil between batches if necessary.

Serve as is, topped with sliced spring onion, or enjoy wrapped in lettuce and perilla leaves, with steamed rice on the side for a more substantial meal.

Spicy stir-fried octopus

Nakji bokkeum

This is a real winter treat for those who like it hot; it's spicy 'Seoul food' at its best. The baby octopus is perfectly cooked in a gochujang hot sauce – just 10 minutes' marinating and then a quick and easy stir-fry, so the flesh is tender and juicy, never tough.

SERVES 2–3

- 300 G (10½ OZ) BABY OCTOPUS (ABOUT 10-12) (SEE NOTES)
- 1 TEASPOON SALT
- 2 TABLESPOONS VEGETABLE OIL
- ½ ONION, THINLY SLICED
- 2 SPRING ONIONS (SCALLIONS), CUT INTO 5 CM (2 IN) LENGTHS, PLUS EXTRA, THINLY SLICED, TO SERVE
- TOASTED SESAME SEEDS, TO SERVE
- STEAMED RICE, TO SERVE

SPICY OCTOPUS MARINADE

- 2 TABLESPOONS GOCHUJANG
- 1 TABLESPOON GOCHUGARU
- 1 TABLESPOON SOY SAUCE
- 1 TABLESPOON CASTER (SUPERFINE) SUGAR
- 1 TABLESPOON KOREAN RICE SYRUP (SSALYEOT) OR CORN SYRUP, GLUCOSE OR HONEY
- 2 TABLESPOONS SESAME OIL
- 1 TABLESPOON TOASTED SESAME SEEDS
- 5 GARLIC CLOVES, FINELY CHOPPED

To prepare the octopus, make a cut between the head and the tentacles. Turn the head inside out, clean out all the innards and trim away the eyes and the beak. Cut the tentacles in half. Put the octopus in a bowl, add the salt, then use your hands to massage the octopus for 2–3 minutes to clean the suction cups. Once tiny bubbles form on the suction cups, rinse the octopus under cold water two or three times, then drain and set aside.

To make the spicy octopus marinade, combine all the ingredients in a bowl and mix until the sugar has dissolved. Add the marinade to the octopus and stir until well coated. Set aside to marinate for 10 minutes.

Heat the vegetable oil in a frying pan or wok over medium–high heat. Stir-fry the onion for 2 minutes or until soft and translucent. Add the marinated octopus, scraping all the marinade from the bowl into the pan. Stir-fry for 3 minutes or until the octopus is just cooked through. Add the spring onion, stir-fry for another 30 seconds, then remove from the heat and transfer to a serving bowl. Garnish with sesame seeds and extra spring onion, and serve immediately with steamed rice.

NOTES / You can substitute octopus with squid, just cut them into bite-sized pieces and score them.

It is very important not to overcook the octopus or it will be rubbery and chewy.

Rice Nood

& les

KOREAN RICE – A SHORT-GRAIN WHITE RICE THAT'S OFTEN A LITTLE ON THE STICKY SIDE – IS SO CENTRAL TO THE FOOD CULTURE THAT THE KOREAN WORD FOR COOKED RICE, 'BAP', IS PRETTY MUCH SYNONYMOUS WITH 'MEAL' OR 'FOOD'. COLOURFUL, COMFORTING BIBIMBAP HAS BECOME A WORLDWIDE FAVOURITE – MY MONEY'S ON KIMCHI FRIED RICE BEING NEXT IN LINE FOR GLOBAL STARDOM.

NOODLES – ALL WITH THEIR OWN SUBTLE FLAVOURS AND BEST USES – ARE MADE FROM A DIZZYING ARRAY OF INGREDIENTS, INCLUDING SWEET POTATO, RICE, WHEAT, BUCKWHEAT AND CORNFLOUR. THEY COME THICK OR THIN, CHEWY OR GLASS-SLIPPERY, IN GENTLE BROTH OR FIERY SAUCE, TRADITIONAL OR MODERN FUSION, COMFORTINGLY HOT OR REFRESHINGLY CHILLED, CHILLI-SPICED OR MILD, FOR EVERY DAY OR FOR FESTIVE DAYS ... THERE TRULY IS A KOREAN NOODLE DISH TO FIT EVERY OCCASION.

Korean mixed rice bowl

Bibimbap

Bibimbap means 'mixed rice' – which very much underplays the satisfying deliciousness on offer here. It's one of Korea's most famous dishes and it's not hard to see why. Typically, a bibimbap is put together by using all the leftover banchan (side dishes) you have sitting in the fridge, so feel free to add as much or as little of each topping as you like. If you ever have leftover bulgogi from the barbecue (page 164), use it here; if not, make this simple pan-fried version.

SERVES 4

- 440 G (2 CUPS) SHORT-GRAIN RICE
- 2 TABLESPOONS VEGETABLE OIL
- 4 EGGS
- BIBIM SAUCE (PAGE 220), TO SERVE

VEGETABLE TOPPINGS

- SEASONED SOYBEAN SPROUTS (PAGE 191)
- SEASONED ENGLISH SPINACH (PAGE 195)
- SAUTEED ZUCCHINI (PAGE 194)
- SAUTEED FERNBRAKE (PAGE 190)
- SAUTEED BELLFLOWER ROOT (PAGE 205)

BEEF BULGOGI

- 220 G (8 OZ) BEEF RIB EYE OR SCOTCH FILLET
- 1 TABLESPOON SOY SAUCE
- 2 TEASPOONS CASTER (SUPERFINE) SUGAR
- 2 TEASPOONS SESAME OIL
- 3 GARLIC CLOVES, FINELY CHOPPED
- 1 TEASPOON TOASTED SESAME SEEDS

Prepare all the vegetable toppings in advance. You can make them a day ahead and refrigerate until ready to use.

Rinse the rice two or three times under cold running water to remove some of the starch. Cook the rice in a rice cooker according to the manufacturer's instructions.

To make the beef bulgogi, slice the beef into 5 mm (¼ in) thick strips and add them to a bowl with the soy sauce, sugar, sesame oil, garlic and sesame seeds. Mix until well combined, then set aside to marinate for 20 minutes.

Heat the vegetable oil in a non-stick frying pan over medium–high heat. Fry the eggs, sunny side up, for about 2 minutes then remove and set aside. In the same pan, stir-fry the beef for 4–5 minutes, until browned and cooked through.

To assemble, place 185 g (1 cup) of cooked rice in each serving bowl. Arrange the vegetable toppings and beef over the rice, then place a fried egg on top. Serve with a big dollop of the bibim sauce on the side.

Kimchi fried rice

Kimchi bokkeum bap

Since you can throw Kimchi fried rice together using nothing but leftovers, it's an amazingly easy and economical dish – yet it still packs a huge flavour punch. This is a traditional favourite with university students who are living on a low budget. If I ever want a home-cooked meal but am feeling too lazy to 'cook', Kimchi fried rice is what always comes to the rescue.

SERVES 2

- 2 TABLESPOONS VEGETABLE OIL
- 2 GARLIC CLOVES, CRUSHED
- 150 G (1 CUP) CABBAGE KIMCHI (PAGE 16), ROUGHLY CHOPPED
- 500 G (1 LB 2 OZ) COOKED SHORT-GRAIN RICE (SEE NOTES)
- 60 ML (¼ CUP) KIMCHI JUICE
- 2 TABLESPOONS GOCHUJANG
- 2 TEASPOONS SESAME OIL
- SALT AND FRESHLY GROUND BLACK PEPPER, TO TASTE
- 1 SPRING ONION (SCALLION), THINLY SLICED
- 2 FRIED EGGS, SUNNY-SIDE UP, TO SERVE

Heat the vegetable oil in a large frying pan or wok over medium–high heat. Add the garlic and stir-fry for 1 minute until fragrant. Add the kimchi and stir-fry for another minute.

Add the rice and use the back of a wooden spoon to break up any clumps. Add the kimchi juice and gochujang and stir-fry for 3–4 minutes, until well combined. Reduce the heat if the rice begins to stick to the base of the pan.

Add the sesame oil and season with salt and pepper to taste. Add half the spring onion, mix well, then divide the fried rice between two bowls. Scatter with the remaining spring onion and top each bowl with a fried egg. Serve immediately.

NOTES / When making fried rice, it is best to cook the rice a day ahead, then refrigerate overnight to draw out any excess moisture. That way, the rice will be drier and easier to cook as opposed to freshly cooked rice, which often turns soggy when you try to stir-fry it.

You can also make a fancy version of this kimchi fried rice by adding thin slices of pork belly, bacon or even SPAM.

BOTTLE

해 제

Sashimi rice bowl

Hoedeopbap

Right here is the perfect lunch for a summer's day when it's too hot to eat a cooked meal! There's very little you need to fuss around with. Simply serve the fresh salad, raw sashimi and sauce on a bed of steamed rice, and then find yourself a shady spot to enjoy it.

SERVES 2

- 220 G (1 CUP) SHORT-GRAIN RICE (SEE NOTES)
- 220 G (8 OZ) FRESH SASHIMI-GRADE SALMON
- 1 CARROT, CUT INTO THIN MATCHSTICKS
- ½ COS (ROMAINE) LETTUCE, THINLY SHREDDED
- ¼ RED ONION, THINLY SLICED
- 1 SPRING ONION (SCALLION), THINLY SLICED
- TOASTED SESAME SEEDS, TO SERVE
- SPICY SEAFOOD SAUCE (PAGE 221), TO SERVE (SEE NOTES)

Cook the rice in a rice cooker according to the manufacturer's instructions.

Slice the salmon into 5 mm (¼ in) thick slices, then wrap in plastic wrap and refrigerate until ready to serve.

To assemble, divide the rice between two serving bowls. Top with the carrot, lettuce and onion, and then place the salmon in the centre. Garnish with the spring onion and sesame seeds, and serve with spicy seafood sauce on the side.

NOTE / It is difficult to cook a small quantity of rice in a rice cooker. The 220 g (1 cup) of rice in this recipe will yield about 555 g (3 cups) of cooked rice. Store the leftover rice in the fridge and use it to make Kimchi fried rice (page 108).

Instead of spicy seafood sauce, you can serve this dish with Spicy soy and spring onion sauce (page 223).

Korean sushi rolls

Gimbap

Gimbap is not meant to be fancy. These sushi rolls are more the thing you'd take to a picnic or enjoy as a quick snack; sometimes you'll even find street-food vendors selling bite-sized versions. The cooked rice used in gimbap is usually plain and unseasoned – I'm veering from tradition by adding a hint of rice vinegar here.

SERVES 6–8

- 440 G (2 CUPS) SHORT-GRAIN RICE
- 60 ML (¼ CUP) RICE VINEGAR
- 1 TABLESPOON CASTER (SUPERFINE) SUGAR
- SALT, TO TASTE
- 1 SHORT CUCUMBER
- 1 BUNCH ENGLISH SPINACH, ROOTS TRIMMED
- 2 TEASPOONS SESAME OIL
- 2 EGGS
- 1 TEASPOON VEGETABLE OIL
- 5 NORI SHEETS
- 5 STRIPS OF PRE-CUT YELLOW PICKLED RADISH (SEE NOTES)
- 5 STRIPS OF PRE-CUT BARBECUED GIMBAP HAM (SEE NOTES)
- 5 STRIPS OF PRE-CUT SEASONED BURDOCK ROOT (SEE NOTES)
- MAYONNAISE, SOY SAUCE AND WASABI, TO SERVE

Cook the rice in a rice cooker according to the manufacturer's instructions.

While the rice is cooking, combine the rice vinegar, sugar and a pinch of salt in a small saucepan and stir over low heat until the sugar has dissolved. Set aside.

Once the rice is cooked, spread it out on a baking tray, sprinkle with the rice vinegar mixture and leave to cool to room temperature.

Cut the cucumber in half lengthways and use a teaspoon to scrape out the seeds. Cut each half lengthways into 5 mm (¼ in) thick strips and set aside.

Bring a saucepan of water to a rolling boil over medium–high heat. Add the spinach and par-boil for 1 minute. Drain and refresh the spinach under cold running water, then squeeze out as much water as possible using your hands, and place the spinach in a bowl. Season with the sesame oil and a pinch of salt, and mix well. Set aside.

Beat the eggs and a pinch of salt in a small bowl. Heat the vegetable oil in a non-stick frying pan over medium–low heat and fry the egg for 2–3 minutes. Once the bottom has set, flip the omelette over and cook for 1 minute on the other side. Once cooked, transfer the omelette to a chopping board and slice into 1 cm (½ in) thick strips.

To assemble, place a nori sheet, shiny side down and with the longer side facing you, on a sushi-rolling mat. Spread about 185 g (1 cup) rice evenly over the nori, leaving a 4 cm (1½ in) edge at the top of the nori sheet.

Place one or two strips each of the cucumber, egg, radish, ham and burdock root along the edge that is closest to you, and top with a few spinach leaves. Be careful not to overfill your sushi roll, or you will have trouble rolling it.

Lift the edge of the mat that is closest to you and roll the nori over the filling away from you. Apply firm pressure to the roll and use your fingers to tuck the filling in as you go. Brush the top edge of the seaweed with a little water, then finish rolling to seal the sushi roll tightly. Repeat with the remaining ingredients to make five rolls.

Cut each roll into 2 cm (¾ in) thick pieces and serve with mayonnaise, soy sauce and wasabi on the side.

NOTES / Yellow pickled radish comes in pre-cut strips or one large chunk. If it is a big chunk, just cut it into 5 mm (¼ in) thick strips.

Barbecued gimbap ham, or smoked fish ham, is commonly used for Korean sushi rolls. You can substitute it with smoked ham or even SPAM.

Seasoned burdock root, yellow pickled radish and barbecued gimbap ham are all available from Korean grocery stores.

Sweet potato glass noodles

Japchae

This is another great dish for feeding a crowd ... for the simple reason that everyone loves Japchae! This has to be Korea's most popular noodle dish – chewy, sweet and slightly slippery glass noodles tossed with juicy strips of beef bulgogi and stir-fried fresh vegetables. The best way to keep the colours bright is to make it like a salad: prepare everything separately and then gently toss together with your hands at the end.

SERVES 4

- 170 G (6 OZ) SWEET POTATO STARCH NOODLES
- VEGETABLE OIL, FOR FRYING
- 1 ONION, THINLY SLICED
- 1 SPRING ONION (SCALLION), CUT INTO 5 CM (2 IN) LENGTHS
- 1 CARROT, CUT INTO THIN MATCHSTICKS
- 4-5 DRIED SHIITAKE MUSHROOMS, SOAKED IN WARM WATER FOR 2-3 HOURS, CUT INTO STRIPS
- 110 G (4 OZ) SOY-MARINATED BARBECUED BEEF (PAGE 164), UNCOOKED
- ½ QUANTITY SEASONED ENGLISH SPINACH (PAGE 195)

DRESSING

- 60 ML (¼ CUP) SOY SAUCE
- 1 TABLESPOON CASTER (SUPERFINE) SUGAR
- 2 TABLESPOONS SESAME OIL
- 2 GARLIC CLOVES, FINELY CHOPPED
- 2 TEASPOONS TOASTED SESAME SEEDS

To make the dressing, whisk together all the ingredients in a small bowl until the sugar has dissolved.

Cut the sweet potato starch noodles in half using a pair of kitchen scissors. Bring a saucepan of water to a rolling boil over high heat. Add the noodles and cook according to the packet instructions until soft and chewy. Drain the noodles and rinse under cold running water until chilled. Combine the noodles with 2 tablespoons of the dressing in a large bowl and mix well.

Heat 1 tablespoon vegetable oil in a large non-stick frying pan or wok over medium heat. Add the noodles and stir-fry for 3–4 minutes, until the noodles are translucent. Return the noodles to the bowl.

In the same pan, heat another tablespoon of oil, add the onion and spring onion and stir-fry for 1 minute, until the onion is a little translucent. Add the carrot and stir-fry for another minute, then transfer to the bowl with the noodles.

Add 1–2 teaspoons of oil to the same pan, add the mushroom and bulgogi, and stir-fry for 2–3 minutes, until the beef has browned. Add to the noodles.

Add the seasoned spinach to the noodle bowl, pour over the remaining dressing, and toss everything together with your hands. Taste and adjust the seasoning accordingly. Divide among serving bowls and serve warm.

Fire noodles

'Buldak ramen'

Here I put my own spin on Korea's famous buldak ramen. Fire noodles can be a great challenge when you're feeding your cocky chilli-fanatic friends, who always start off saying: 'This isn't too hot!' Make a rule that no one's allowed to touch their glass of milk until they've finished all the noodles in the bowl!

SERVES 2

- 2 PACKETS INSTANT RAMEN OR UDON NOODLES
- LARGE HANDFUL OF SHREDDED ICEBERG LETTUCE LEAVES (OPTIONAL)
- FRIED SHALLOTS, TO SERVE
- 2 EGGS, FRIED SUNNY SIDE UP
- GLASSES OF MILK, ON STANDBY

FIRE NOODLE SAUCE

- 1 TABLESPOON VEGETABLE OIL
- 2 TABLESPOONS GOCHUJANG
- 2 TEASPOONS KOREAN CAPSAICIN HOT SAUCE
- 2 TABLESPOONS LIGHT SOY SAUCE
- 1 TABLESPOON DARK SOY SAUCE
- 2 TEASPOONS RICE VINEGAR
- 3 GARLIC CLOVES, MINCED
- 2.5 CM (1 IN) PIECE OF GINGER, PEELED AND GRATED
- 2 TEASPOONS SESAME OIL
- 1 TABLESPOON CASTER (SUPERFINE) SUGAR

To make the fire noodle sauce, combine all the ingredients in a bowl and stir until the sugar has dissolved. Set aside.

Cook the instant noodles according to the packet instructions, then drain, saving 125 ml (½ cup) of the cooking water. Divide the noodles between two serving bowls.

Add 2 tablespoons of the fire noodle sauce to each bowl and toss until the noodles are well coated. Top with the shredded lettuce (if using) and fried shallots, and finish with the fried eggs.

Serve with glasses of milk to reduce the burn!

Spicy cold buckwheat noodles

Bibim naengmyeon

This is the spicy version of Naengmyeon (page 126). Instead of being served in a broth, bibim naengmyeon noodles are served with a fiery gochujang sauce. The idea is that eating spicy food will make you perspire, which helps cool your body down – and this is indeed surprisingly refreshing on a hot day.

SERVES 4

- 625 G (1 LB 6 OZ) DRIED BUCKWHEAT NOODLES
- PICKLED CUCUMBER (PAGE 127) AND PICKLED RADISH (PAGE 127), TO SERVE
- 4 HARD-BOILED EGGS, HALVED
- TOASTED SESAME SEEDS, TO SERVE

BEEF BROTH

- 300 G (10½ OZ) BEEF BRISKET
- ½ ONION, UNPEELED, HALVED
- 1 GREEN APPLE, HALVED
- 5 GARLIC CLOVES, PEELED
- 30 G (1 OZ) SLICED GINGER
- 1 TEASPOON BLACK PEPPERCORNS
- 2 SPRING ONIONS (SCALLIONS), WHITE PARTS ONLY
- 1 TEASPOON SALT

SPICY SAUCE

- ½ NASHI OR ASIAN PEAR, CORED
- ½ ONION, PEELED
- 2 GARLIC CLOVES
- 30 G (¼ CUP) GOCHUGARU
- 2 TABLESPOONS GOCHUJANG
- 1 TABLESPOON SUGAR
- 1 TABLESPOON FISH SAUCE
- 2 TABLESPOONS WHITE VINEGAR
- 2 TEASPOONS SESAME OIL

To make the beef broth, combine all the ingredients in a large stockpot. Add 3 litres (3 quarts) of water and bring to the boil over high heat. Skim off any impurities that rise to the surface, then reduce the heat to medium–low. Cover with a lid (leaving it slightly ajar) and simmer for 1 hour, until the beef is tender. Remove the beef from the stock and set aside to cool to room temperature. Wrap the beef in plastic wrap and chill in the fridge for at least 4 hours, or preferably overnight.

Strain the broth through a fine-mesh sieve into a large airtight container. Reserve 60 ml (¼ cup) of the broth to make the spicy sauce. Keep the remaining broth to make the chilled buckwheat noodle soup on page 126.

To make the spicy sauce, combine all the ingredients and the reserved broth in a food processor and blend to a fine puree. Refrigerate until needed.

Take the beef out of the fridge and slice it thinly against the grain.

Cook the noodles according to the packet instructions. Prepare an ice bath while the noodles are cooking. Once cooked, drain the noodles and immediately plunge them into the iced water to stop the cooking process. Drain, and place the noodles in a bowl.

Add the spicy sauce and toss until the noodles are well coated. Divide the noodles among four serving bowls and top each with some pickled cucumber and radish, a few slices of beef and a boiled egg. Sprinkle sesame seeds over the top and serve.

Spicy mixed noodles

Bibim guksu

Same same, but actually very different. This is similar to Bibim naengmyeon (page 122), but uses long, thin wheat noodles instead of buckwheat noodles and is tossed together with fewer ingredients. When you need to quickly rustle up a big bowl of spicy noodles to feed a crowd, this recipe will gain you a reputation as a kitchen magician.

SERVES 2

- 200 G (7 OZ) THIN WHEAT FLOUR NOODLES (SOMYEON)
- 75 G (½ CUP) CABBAGE KIMCHI (PAGE 16), FINELY CHOPPED
- ½ SHORT CUCUMBER, CUT INTO MATCHSTICKS
- 1 HARD-BOILED EGG, HALVED
- TOASTED SESAME SEEDS, TO SERVE

SPICY SAUCE

- 60 ML (¼ CUP) KIMCHI JUICE
- 2 TABLESPOONS GOCHUJANG
- 1 GARLIC CLOVE, FINELY CHOPPED
- 2 TEASPOONS SESAME OIL
- 2 TEASPOONS WHITE VINEGAR
- 1 TABLESPOON SUGAR
- 1 TABLESPOON TOASTED SESAME SEEDS

To make the spicy sauce, combine all the ingredients in a bowl and mix until the sugar has dissolved. Refrigerate until ready to use.

Prepare a large bowl of iced water and set aside. Bring a large saucepan of water to the boil over high heat. Cook the wheat flour noodles according to the packet instructions. Drain, then immediately refresh the noodles in the iced water to stop the cooking process. Leave to chill for 2–3 minutes. Briefly stir the noodles around in the water to loosen them up, then drain.

Transfer the noodles to a large bowl, add the kimchi and spicy sauce and mix until the noodles are well coated in the sauce. Divide the noodles between two serving bowls. Top with the cucumber, half a hard-boiled egg, and sprinkle with sesame seeds to garnish. Serve immediately.

NOTE / Typically, Bibim guksu is a vegetarian dish. You can make it more substantial by adding lettuce leaves, thinly sliced carrot or shredded cabbage.

Chilled buckwheat noodle soup

Naengmyeon

Just the thing for a hot summer's day, naengmyeon is a bowl of noodles in a refreshingly tart and tangy chilled beef broth. Traditionally, the long noodles are eaten without being cut – to symbolise good health and longevity. So, take a deep breath and get ready to slurp! If you prefer your noodles with a bit of heat, check out the recipe for Bibim naengmyeon (page 122).

SERVES 4

- 625 G (1 LB 6 OZ) BUCKWHEAT NOODLES
- 2 HARD-BOILED EGGS, HALVED
- HOT ENGLISH MUSTARD, TO SERVE

BEEF BROTH

- 300 G (10½ OZ) BEEF BRISKET
- ½ ONION, UNPEELED, HALVED
- 1 GREEN APPLE, HALVED
- 5 GARLIC CLOVES, PEELED
- 2 CM (¾ IN) PIECE OF GINGER, THINLY SLICED
- 1 TEASPOON BLACK PEPPERCORNS
- 2 SPRING ONIONS (SCALLIONS), WHITE PARTS ONLY
- 1 TEASPOON SALT

SOUP BASE

- 2 TABLESPOONS SOY SAUCE
- 125 ML (½ CUP) WHITE VINEGAR
- 60 G (2 OZ) CASTER (SUPERFINE) SUGAR
- 3 TEASPOONS SALT
- 500 ML (2 CUPS) RADISH WATER KIMCHI BROTH (PAGE 22) (OPTIONAL; SEE NOTES)

To make the beef broth, combine all the ingredients in a large stockpot. Add 3 litres (3 quarts) of water and bring to the boil over high heat. Skim off any impurities that rise to the surface, then reduce the heat to medium–low. Cover with a lid (leaving it slightly ajar) and simmer for 1 hour or until the beef is tender. Remove the beef from the stock and allow the beef and stock to cool to room temperature. Wrap the beef in plastic wrap and chill in the fridge for at least 4 hours, or preferably overnight.

Strain the broth through a fine-mesh sieve into a large airtight container. Add all the ingredients for the soup base and stir until the sugar has dissolved. The soup should taste sharp, tart and mildly sweet. Taste and adjust the seasoning if necessary. Seal the container with a lid, and transfer to the fridge to chill for at least 4 hours, or preferably overnight. To speed up the chilling process, you can place the stock in the freezer for 1–2 hours, until it becomes slushy but not frozen.

To make the pickled cucumber, cut the cucumber in half lengthways then slice each half on an angle into 3 mm (⅛ in) thick slices. Transfer to a bowl, then add the salt and sugar. Toss to combine, leave to sit for 10 minutes, then add the vinegar and mix well. Refrigerate until ready to use.

For the pickled radishes, thinly slice the radish then stack the slices up and cut into 2 cm (¾ in) wide strips. Transfer to a bowl, then add the salt and sugar. Toss to combine, leave to sit for 10 minutes, then add the vinegar and mix well. Refrigerate until ready to use.

PICKLED CUCUMBER

- 1 SHORT CUCUMBER
- ¼ TEASPOON SALT
- 2 TEASPOONS CASTER (SUPERFINE) SUGAR
- 2 TABLESPOONS WHITE VINEGAR

PICKLED RADISH

- 200 G (7 OZ) KOREAN RADISH, PEELED
- ¼ TEASPOON SALT
- 2 TEASPOONS CASTER (SUPERFINE) SUGAR
- 2 TABLESPOONS WHITE VINEGAR

Take the beef out of the fridge and slice it thinly against the grain.

Cook the buckwheat noodles according to the packet instructions. Prepare an ice bath while the noodles are cooking. Once cooked, drain the noodles and immediately plunge them into the iced water to stop the cooking process. Drain, and divide the noodles among four bowls.

To each bowl, add some pickled cucumber and radish, a few slices of beef and half a boiled egg. Divide the chilled soup among the bowls. Serve cold with hot mustard.

NOTES / If using radish water kimchi broth in the soup base, simply replace 500 ml (2 cups) of the beef stock with the broth and use less vinegar and salt in the soup.

For this noodle dish, you can also add a few slices of Nashi or Asian pear if they are in season.

特選
特選特
選特
特選

Festive noodle soup

Janchi guksu

Janchi guksu means 'banquet dish' and, traditionally, this is made for special occasions such as wedding feasts, birthday parties and festive holidays. But let's just agree that every day can be a holiday when you have a big bowl of festive noodle soup to warm body and soul!

SERVES 4

- 1 ZUCCHINI (COURGETTE)
- 1 TEASPOON SALT, PLUS EXTRA FOR SAUTEING
- 60 ML (¼ CUP) VEGETABLE OIL
- 1 BUNCH ENGLISH SPINACH, RINSED AND CUT INTO 5 CM (2 IN) LENGTHS
- 2 EGGS, BEATEN
- ANCHOVY AND KELP STOCK (PAGE 230)
- 450 G (1 LB) THIN WHEAT FLOUR NOODLES (SOMYEON)
- 1 TEASPOON TOASTED SESAME SEEDS
- SPICY SOY AND SPRING ONION SAUCE (PAGE 223), TO SERVE

Cut the zucchini in half lengthways, then cut each half on an angle into thin 3 mm (⅛ in) slices. Combine the sliced zucchini and salt in a bowl, mix well, and set aside for 10 minutes. Use your hands to squeeze out as much liquid as possible from the zucchini.

Heat 1 tablespoon of the vegetable oil in a frying pan over medium heat and saute the zucchini for 1–2 minutes, until softened. Transfer to a plate.

Heat another tablespoon of the oil in the same frying pan and cook the spinach for 1 minute, until softened. Season to taste with salt and stir-fry for another minute, then transfer to the plate with the zucchini.

Heat the remaining oil in the same frying pan, add the beaten egg, then swirl the pan around to spread the egg into a thin layer. Fry for 2 minutes, then flip the omelette over and fry for another minute or until lightly golden. Transfer the omelette to a chopping board and cut into thin strips. Transfer to the plate with the spinach and zucchini.

Bring the anchovy and kelp stock to a simmer over low heat, ready for serving.

Prepare a large bowl of iced water and set aside.

Bring a large saucepan of water to the boil over high heat and cook the wheat flour noodles according to the packet instructions. Drain, then immediately refresh in the iced water to stop the cooking process. Leave to chill for 2–3 minutes. Briefly stir the noodles around in the water to loosen them up, then drain.

Divide the noodles among four serving bowls. Pour ladles of hot stock into each bowl, then top the noodles with the zucchini, spinach and egg. Garnish with sesame seeds and serve with spicy soy and spring onion sauce on the side.

국물

Soups & Stews

A BOWL OF SOUP IS VIEWED AS THE ULTIMATE COMFORT IN MANY FOOD CULTURES, ESPECIALLY IF YOU'RE NOT FEELING WELL OR NEED TO BANISH THE WINTER CHILLS. KOREA IS NO EXCEPTION – A DELICIOUS ARRAY OF BOLD AND NOURISHING SOUPS PROMISES TO CURE ANY AILMENTS OF THE SOUL.

AND IS THERE ANY BETTER MEAL FOR BRINGING FRIENDS AND FAMILY TOGETHER THAN A SPICY ONE-POT WONDER, FROM THE SIMPLEST OF EVERYDAY KIMCHI STEWS TO A GLORIOUS BUBBLING CLAYPOT OF SEAFOOD AND SILKEN TOFU IN FIERY RED SAUCE? ANY HOTPOT DINNERTIME CAN'T HELP BUT TURN INTO A JOYFUL COMMUNAL AFFAIR, WHERE EVERYONE JUST DIGS IN WITHOUT CEREMONY AND FISHES ALL THE DELICIOUS GOODIES FROM THE POT.

Soybean sprout soup

Kongnamul guk

Kongnamul guk is the epitome of home-cooked comfort, a good example of the simplest dishes sometimes being the best. This is an everyday soup that most households sit down to as part of a family dinner. Add a sprinkling of gochugaru if you'd like to spice things up a little. And be careful not to overcook the sprouts – you want them to keep their crunch.

SERVES 4

- 1 × QUANTITY ANCHOVY & KELP STOCK (PAGE 230)
- 250 G (9 OZ) SOYBEAN SPROUTS
- 1 GARLIC CLOVE, FINELY CHOPPED
- 2 TABLESPOONS FISH SAUCE
- SALT, TO TASTE
- 1 SPRING ONION (SCALLION), THINLY SLICED
- 2 BIRD'S EYE CHILLIES, THINLY SLICED

Bring the stock to the boil over high heat. Rinse the bean sprouts and discard any spoiled sprouts. Add to the stock, cover with a lid and reduce the heat to medium. Cook for 10 minutes.

Add the garlic, fish sauce and season to taste with salt. Simmer for a further 5 minutes.

Ladle the bean sprouts and broth into individual bowls and garnish with spring onion and chilli. Serve hot.

Seaweed and beef soup

Miyeok guk

This nourishing soup is associated with birth in Korean culture: it's often eaten on birthdays and is traditionally made for new mums to replenish the body. As well as the fortifying beef, miyeok seaweed – wakame in Japanese cooking – is rich in umami flavour and essential nutrients.

SERVES 4–6

- 40 G (1 CUP) DRIED WAKAME SEAWEED
- 150 G (5½ OZ) GRAVY BEEF, BRISKET OR SHANK, THINLY SLICED
- 2 GARLIC CLOVES, FINELY CHOPPED
- 2 TABLESPOONS SOY SAUCE

Soak the dried seaweed in a large bowl of cold water for 30 minutes. Drain and rinse under cold running water two or three times, rubbing the seaweed with your hands to remove any excess salt. Drain and squeeze out as much water as possible. You should have about 120 g (3 cups) seaweed once it has been rehydrated. Cut the seaweed into bite-sized pieces and set aside.

Combine the sliced beef and 2.5 litres (2½ quarts) of water in a large stockpot and bring to a rolling boil over high heat. Skim off any impurities that rise to the surface. Reduce the heat to medium–low, cover with a lid (leaving it slightly ajar) and simmer for 30 minutes. Add the chopped seaweed, garlic and soy sauce and simmer for a further 10 minutes, until the beef is tender. Taste and adjust the seasoning if necessary.

Divide the soup among bowls and serve.

Potato and dumpling soup

Sujebi

Sujebi could be viewed as Korea's version of Italy's minestrone. This is a wholesome, comforting soup, packed with potatoes and hand-torn dumplings. The dumpling noodles are soft and chewy, and the broth is rich with umami flavour. It's a big warm hug in a bowl – perfect for cold weather.

SERVES 4

CABBAGE KIMCHI (PAGE 16), TO SERVE

DUMPLING DOUGH

- 150 G (1 CUP) PLAIN (ALL-PURPOSE) FLOUR, PLUS EXTRA FOR DUSTING
- 1 EGG
- 1 TABLESPOON VEGETABLE OIL
- ½ TEASPOON SALT

POTATO SOUP

- 3 FLOURY POTATOES, SUCH AS RUSSETS OR COLIBANS
- 1 × QUANTITY ANCHOVY AND KELP STOCK (PAGE 230)
- 1 TABLESPOON FISH SAUCE
- 2 SPRING ONIONS (SCALLIONS), CUT INTO 5 CM (2 IN) LENGTHS

To make the dumpling dough, put the flour in a large bowl and make a well in the centre. Add the remaining ingredients and, using a fork, slowly bring everything together to form a soft dough, adding a little water to the mixture if it seems dry. Transfer the dough to a lightly floured work surface and knead for at least 5 minutes, until the dough is smooth and elastic. Form the dough into a ball and wrap in plastic wrap. Refrigerate until ready to use.

To make the potato soup, peel the potatoes and cut into 1 cm (½ in) cubes. Combine the potato and stock in a large saucepan and bring to the boil over medium–high heat. Unwrap the dough and, holding it in one hand, pinch and stretch a small piece of dough from the ball until you have a small 3–4 cm (1¼–1½ in) piece. Tear it off and drop it into the boiling stock. Repeat with the remaining dough.

Cook for 2–3 minutes, stirring occasionally. The dumplings are cooked when they float to the surface. Season with the fish sauce, add the spring onion and mix well. Taste and adjust the seasoning if necessary.

Ladle the soup into individual bowls and serve hot with the cabbage kimchi.

Fermented soybean hotpot

Doenjang jjigae

This deliciously funky hotpot never fails to please and is generally craved as the ultimate in hearty, comfort food. Doenjang jjigae seems to be a particular home-cooked favourite of Korean men, especially of the older generations. The fermented soybean paste has a strong earthy flavour, a little like miso, and the tofu, enoki mushrooms and zucchini soak it up like champs.

SERVES 2

- 2 ZUCCHINI (COURGETTES)
- 100 G (3½ OZ) ENOKI MUSHROOMS
- 1 LITRE (4 CUPS) ANCHOVY AND KELP STOCK (PAGE 230) (SEE NOTE)
- 160 G (5½ OZ) KOREAN FERMENTED SOYBEAN PASTE (DOENJANG)
- 2 TEASPOONS GOCHUGARU
- 150 G (5½ OZ) MEDIUM-FIRM TOFU, CUT INTO 2 CM (¾ IN) CUBES
- 1 SPRING ONION (SCALLION), THINLY SLICED

Top and tail the zucchini, then cut them in half lengthways. Slice into 1 cm (½ in) thick slices. Trim the roots off the enoki mushrooms and brush off any dirt. Set aside.

Pour the anchovy and kelp stock into a Korean stone bowl pot (dolsot) or claypot and bring to a simmer over medium–high heat. Put the soybean paste in a fine-mesh sieve and use the back of a spoon to push the paste through the mesh into the stock. Stir until the paste has dissolved.

Add the gochugaru, zucchini and tofu and bring to the boil for 5 minutes or until the zucchini is soft. Add the enoki mushrooms and spring onion, and boil for another minute. Taste and adjust the seasoning if necessary.

Serve the stew bubbling away in the pot, with steamed rice on the side.

Spicy chicken and potato stew

Dak tori tang

Dak tori tang (also called Dak bokkeum tang) is a deceptively simple braised chicken stew with potatoes and carrots. Typically, a whole chicken is used, but I make this with wings and thighs for easy eating – it also saves the hassle of cutting up and marinating a whole chicken. Braise the chicken nice and slow in the spicy red sauce and you'll be rewarded with succulent, tender meat and silky soft potatoes.

SERVES 4

- 1 KG (2 LB 3 OZ) CHICKEN WINGS OR THIGH FILLETS
- 1 ONION, PEELED AND QUARTERED
- 300 G (10½ OZ) FLOURY POTATOES, SUCH AS RUSSETS OR COLIBANS, PEELED AND QUARTERED
- 2 CARROTS, CUT INTO LARGE CHUNKS
- 1 SPRING ONION (SCALLION), THINLY SLICED

SPICY SAUCE

- 70 G (¼ CUP) GOCHUJANG
- 2 TABLESPOONS GOCHUGARU
- 5 GARLIC CLOVES, FINELY CHOPPED
- 1 TABLESPOON CASTER (SUPERFINE) SUGAR
- 60 ML (¼ CUP) SOY SAUCE
- 2 TABLESPOONS MIRIN
- 1 TABLESPOON KOREAN RICE SYRUP (SSALYEOT) OR CORN SYRUP, GLUCOSE OR HONEY
- 1 TABLESPOON SESAME OIL

If using chicken wings, separate them into three parts: the meaty drumette, the wingette and the tip. Discard the tips or reserve them for another recipe. If using chicken thigh fillets, cut the chicken into bite-sized pieces. Place the chicken in a large bowl and set aside

To make the spicy sauce, combine all the ingredients in a large saucepan and stir until combined. Add the chicken and onion and use your hands (wear food preparation gloves if necessary) to rub the marinade into the meat and onion until well coated.

Add 250 ml (1 cup) of water to the marinade and chicken and stir well. Place the pan over medium–high heat and bring to the boil. Cover with a lid and simmer, stirring occasionally, for 20 minutes or until the chicken is cooked.

Stir in the potato and carrot, cover with the lid, then reduce the heat to medium and cook for a further 20 minutes or until the chicken is tender and the potato is soft. Remove the lid and continue simmering for a further 10 minutes or until the sauce has reduced slightly.

Transfer the stew to a serving bowl and serve hot, garnished with the spring onion. Serve simply with steamed rice and a few dishes from the Banchan chapter (pages 190–215).

Kimchi stew

Kimchi jjigae

When your jar of kimchi has been sitting in the fridge for months and has started to taste a little sour, it's reached its peak moment in life: it's now perfect for making Kimchi stew! This simple, warming, hearty dish always hits the spot. Just as kimchi is the national favourite, it's hard to find anyone who doesn't love Kimchi jjigae.

SERVES 2

- 1 TABLESPOON VEGETABLE OIL
- 300 G (2 CUPS) CABBAGE KIMCHI (PAGE 16), ROUGHLY CHOPPED
- 2 GARLIC CLOVES, FINELY CHOPPED
- 60 ML (¼ CUP) KIMCHI JUICE
- 2 TABLESPOONS GOCHUGARU
- 1 TABLESPOON FISH SAUCE
- 150 G (5½ OZ) FIRM TOFU, CUT INTO 2 CM (¾ IN) CUBES
- THINLY SLICED SPRING ONION (SCALLION), TO SERVE

Heat the vegetable oil in a Korean stone bowl pot (dolsot) or claypot over medium–high heat. Add the kimchi and garlic and fry for 2–3 minutes, until softened. Add the kimchi juice, gochugaru and fish sauce, then pour in 1 litre (4 cups) of water. Stir, and bring to the boil.

Add the tofu, cover with a lid, and reduce the heat to medium–low. Simmer for 10 minutes, then taste and adjust the seasoning if necessary. Serve the stew still bubbling away in the pot, topped with spring onion and with steamed rice on the side.

Pork rib kimchi stew

Daeji galbi kimchi jjigae

Adding pork ribs to an everyday basic kimchi stew turns it into something even more substantial and special. The ribs give a fantastic depth of flavour and the longer and more slowly you simmer them, the more tender they will get, until the meat is falling off the bone.

SERVES 2

- 500 G (1 LB 2 OZ) PORK SHORT RIBS
- 1 TABLESPOON VEGETABLE OIL
- 300 G (2 CUPS) CABBAGE KIMCHI (PAGE 16), ROUGHLY CHOPPED
- 2 GARLIC CLOVES, FINELY CHOPPED
- 2 TABLESPOONS KIMCHI JUICE
- 2 TABLESPOONS GOCHUGARU
- 2 TABLESPOONS FISH SAUCE
- 150 G (5½ OZ) FIRM TOFU, CUT INTO 2 CM (¾ IN) CUBES
- THINLY SLICED SPRING ONION (SCALLION), TO SERVE

Cut the pork between the ribs into bite-sized pieces and soak in a bowl of cold water for 1 hour. Transfer the ribs to a large saucepan, cover with water and bring to a rolling boil over high heat. Boil for 3 minutes, then drain and rinse the ribs under cold running water to remove any impurities. Set aside.

Heat the vegetable oil in a Korean stone bowl pot (dolsot) or claypot over medium–high heat and fry the kimchi and garlic for 2–3 minutes, until softened. Add the kimchi juice, gochugaru and fish sauce, then pour in 1 litre (4 cups) of water. Stir, and bring to the boil.

Add the pork ribs, stir to mix well, then reduce the heat to a very low simmer and cook, covered, for 1–2 hours, until the pork is tender. Add the tofu and simmer for another 10 minutes. Taste and adjust the seasoning if necessary.

Serve the stew still bubbling away in the pot, topped with spring onion and with steamed rice on the side.

Spicy silken tofu hotpot

Sundubu jjigae

There are few sights more warming to the hungry soul than a bubbling hotpot filled with seafood and silken tofu in a red-hot spicy soup. I love the wonderful play of textures here – the silky-smooth tofu, the springy bite of the seafood and the soft zucchini.

SERVES 2

- 1 ZUCCHINI (COURGETTE)
- 100 G (3½ OZ) ENOKI MUSHROOMS
- 300 ML (10 FL OZ) ANCHOVY AND KELP STOCK (PAGE 230)
- 30 G (¼ CUP) GOCHUGARU, OR TO TASTE
- 60 ML (¼ CUP) FISH SAUCE
- 200 G (7 OZ) MIXED SEAFOOD (PRAWNS/SHRIMP, SCALLOPS, MUSSELS, CALAMARI)
- 500 G (1 LB 2 OZ) SILKEN TOFU
- 1 SPRING ONION (SCALLION), THINLY SLICED
- 1 TEASPOON SESAME OIL
- 1 EGG

Top and tail the zucchini, cut in half lengthways, then cut into 1 cm (½ in) thick slices. Trim the roots off the enoki mushrooms and brush off any dirt. Set aside.

Bring the stock to the boil in a Korean stone bowl pot (dolsot) or claypot over medium–high heat. Add the gochugaru and fish sauce, and stir to mix well. Add the zucchini and mixed seafood and boil for 3 minutes, until the zucchini has softened slightly. Add the silken tofu and use a spoon to break it into smaller pieces. Reduce the heat to medium–low and simmer for 2 minutes. Taste and adjust the seasoning if necessary, adding more gochugaru if you want the stew extra hot!

Remove from the heat, add the spring onion and sesame oil and gently stir to combine. Gently crack the egg into the centre of the pot and serve the stew while it is still bubbling. At the table, break the yolk with chopsticks and stir it into the soup, then dig in.

Army base stew

Budae jjigae

This extremely spicy bowl of blistering goodness was created soon after the armistice that ended the Korean War, using ingredients that were scrounged or smuggled off the US army bases, hence its nickname: 'army base stew'.

SERVES 4–6

- 50 G (1¾ OZ) FROZEN TTEOK (KOREAN TUBULAR RICE CAKES)
- 200 G (1 CUP) CABBAGE KIMCHI
- 200 G (7 OZ) SPAM
- 2 HOTDOG FRANKFURTERS
- 300 G (10½ OZ) FIRM TOFU
- 200 G (7 OZ) SHIITAKE MUSHROOMS
- 50 G (1¾ OZ) ENOKI MUSHROOMS
- 1 LITRE (4 CUPS) CHICKEN STOCK
- 2 SPRING ONIONS (SCALLIONS), THINLY SLICED
- 110 G (4 OZ) INSTANT RAMEN NOODLES
- 1-2 KRAFT SINGLES
- STEAMED RICE, TO SERVE

BUDAE JJIGAE CHILLI PASTE

- 3 GARLIC CLOVES, MINCED
- 2 TABLESPOONS GOCHUGARU
- 1 TABLESPOON GOCHUJANG
- 2 TABLESPOONS MIRIN RICE WINE
- 1 TABLESPOON SOY SAUCE
- 1 TEASPOON SESAME OIL
- 2 TEASPOONS SUGAR

Soak the frozen tteok in warm water for 20 minutes until soft, then drain and set aside.

Meanwhile, to make the budae jjigae chilli paste, combine all the ingredients in a bowl and stir until the sugar has dissolved. Set aside.

Roughly chop the kimchi and thinly slice the SPAM, frankfurters, tofu and shiitake mushrooms. Trim the base of the enoki mushrooms.

Arrange the kimchi, SPAM, frankfurter, tofu , shiitake and enoki mushrooms and tteok around the base of a shallow flameproof casserole dish. Spoon the chilli paste into the centre of the dish, then pour the stock around the chilli paste. Cover, then bring to the boil over medium–high heat and cook for 5–8 minutes.

Gently stir the chilli paste into the broth and sprinkle the spring onion over the top. Place the ramen noodles in the dish, then place the cheese slices on top of the noodles. Let the stew simmer for 2–3 minutes, until the noodles are cooked. Remove from the heat and take the dish to the table.

If you have a portable gas burner, serve the hot stew over the burner at the table so it remains steaming hot.

Serve the stew with steamed rice to soak up that spicy sauce.

Mix 'n' Feasts

Match

TRADITIONAL KOREAN BARBECUE IS EASY TO FALL FOR. THE NOVELTY OF HANDS-ON GRILLING OVER SMOKING HOT CHARCOAL RIGHT AT THE TABLE ALWAYS MAKES FOR A FUN DINING EXPERIENCE. IT'S ALSO PERFECT FOR STRESS-FREE SUMMER BARBECUE ENTERTAINING AT HOME – STRESS-FREE BECAUSE YOU CAN JUST SET IT ALL UP AT THE TABLE AND ASK EVERYONE TO GRILL THE MEAT THEMSELVES.

DEPENDING ON THE NUMBER OF DINERS, YOU MIGHT WANT TO MIX-AND-MATCH TWO OR THREE DIFFERENT CHOICES. BULGOGI IS A MUST AT ANY BARBECUE – THE THINLY SLICED BEEF IS MARINATED IN A SWEET SOY SAUCE THAT STARTS TO CARAMELISE AS SOON AS IT HITS THE GRILL. IMBUED WITH THE SMOKY FLAVOUR FROM THE CHARCOAL, IT'S HARD TO BEAT. PAIR THE GRILLED MEAT WITH A BRAISE (JJIM) OR TWO THAT YOU CAN EASILY MAKE AHEAD. PERHAPS THE GENTLE BRAISED SNAPPER, SOY-BRAISED CHICKEN WINGS OR TOFU?

ADD A BOWL OF STEAMED RICE, A FEW BANCHAN FROM THE NEXT CHAPTER AND SOME DIPPING SAUCES AND/OR KIMCHI, AND LET THE FEASTING BEGIN!

TM2000
OFF

Barbecued beef short ribs

Galbi

Nicknamed 'the king of all Korean barbecue', galbi is a favourite at any gathering around the grill. The ingenious way of filleting the meat from the rib in a long thin strip – but leaving it still attached to the bone – means the beef cooks very quickly and stays juicy. It takes some practice to fillet the rib, but this is an impressive art worth mastering: so, take your time and treat it with care.

SERVES 4–6

- 1 KG (2 LB 3 OZ) BEEF SHORT RIBS
- SOY AND WASABI DIPPING SAUCE (PAGE 226), TO SERVE

BEEF SHORT RIBS MARINADE

- ½ ONION, PEELED
- 1 NASHI OR ASIAN PEAR, PEELED AND CORED
- 5 GARLIC CLOVES, FINELY CHOPPED
- 2 CM (¾ IN) PIECE OF GINGER, PEELED AND FINELY GRATED
- 2 TABLESPOONS CASTER (SUPERFINE) SUGAR
- 60 ML (¼ CUP) SOY SAUCE
- 60 ML (¼ CUP) MIRIN
- 2 TABLESPOONS SESAME OIL
- ¼ TEASPOON FRESHLY GROUND BLACK PEPPER

Trim any fat and silver skin from the ribs, then cut the beef between the ribs into individual pieces. Place a rib, bone side down, on a chopping board. Starting from one side of the rib, carefully tease the meat away from the bone with a very sharp knife without separating it completely. Leave one end of the meat still attached to the bone like a hinge. Open out the meat from the rib (like opening a book), and butterfly the meat part into a long, flat strip, about 5 mm (¼ in) thick. Repeat with the remaining rib pieces then place them in a large bowl.

To make the marinade, combine all the ingredients in a food processor and blend to a puree. Pour the marinade over the ribs and mix well using your hands.

Take a rib bone, roll the meat back around the bone into a scroll, then place it back in the bowl. Repeat with the remaining ribs, so they are sitting neat and tidy in the marinade. Cover the bowl with plastic wrap and transfer to the fridge to marinate for 2 hours, or preferably overnight.

Take the ribs out of the fridge at least 1 hour prior to cooking to allow them to come to room temperature. Set up a Korean barbecue grill plate on a portable gas stove in the centre of the dining table, or set a chargrill pan over high heat. Place the rib pieces on the grill, unrolling them into long strips so they cook evenly. Grill the meat, turning occasionally, for 2–3 minutes, until slightly charred and caramelised on each side.

Cut the meat into bite-sized chunks with a pair of kitchen scissors. Serve immediately with the soy and wasabi dipping sauce.

NOTE / If you prefer, you can also wrap the meat in a cos (romaine) lettuce leaf with a little sliced raw garlic and a drizzle of Spicy dipping sauce (page 222), which is similar to Braised pork belly wraps (page 176).

Soy-marinated barbecued beef

Bulgogi

Bulgogi is a must at any Korean barbecue – the thinly sliced beef is marinated in a sweet soy marinade that starts to caramelise as soon as it hits the grill. Add the smoky flavour of the barbecue and it's easy to see why this has become a global foodie superstar.

SERVES 4–6

- 1 KG (2 LB 3 OZ) BEEF TENDERLOIN OR RIB EYE (SEE NOTE)
- 1 ONION, SLICED (OPTIONAL)
- 3 SPRING ONIONS (SCALLIONS), CUT INTO 5 CM (2 IN) LENGTHS
- TOASTED SESAME SEEDS, TO SERVE
- SPICY DIPPING SAUCE (PAGE 222), TO SERVE

SWEET SOY MARINADE

- 5 GARLIC CLOVES, CRUSHED
- 2 TABLESPOONS CASTER (SUPERFINE) SUGAR
- 60 ML (¼ CUP) SOY SAUCE
- 2 TABLESPOONS MIRIN
- 1 TABLESPOON SESAME OIL
- 1 TEASPOON FRESHLY GROUND BLACK PEPPER

Cut the beef in half lengthways into two long strips, then slice each half against the grain into 3 mm (⅛ in) thick slices. Combine the beef slices, onion (if using) and spring onion in a large bowl and set aside.

To make the marinade, put all the ingredients in a bowl and stir until the sugar has dissolved. Pour the marinade over the beef and, using your hands, mix until well combined. Cover with plastic wrap and leave to marinate in the fridge for at least 1 hour.

Set up a Korean barbecue grill plate on a portable gas stove in the centre of the dining table, or set a chargrill pan over high heat. Working in batches, chargrill the beef for 1–2 minutes each side until caramelised.

Serve the barbecued beef sprinkled with toasted sesame seeds and with the spicy dipping sauce and a big bowl of steamed rice on the side.

NOTE / If you freeze your beef for about 1 hour before slicing it, it will be much easier to cut thinly.

Spicy barbecued pork

Daeji bulgogi

Daeji bulgogi – pork slices marinated in a sweet and spicy sauce – is a great alternative or addition to beef Bulgogi (page 164) at a barbecue gathering. It's always best made with pork that is a little bit fatty, such as belly or shoulder – the fat will render and quickly crisp and caramelise, turning into irresistibly smoky pork crackling.

Serve simply, with steamed rice and banchan, or wrap the spicy pork in crisp cos (romaine) lettuce leaves. (This is also great for handing round as a snack with drinks.)

SERVES 4–6

- 1.5 KG (3 LB 5 OZ) SKINLESS PORK BELLY, CUT INTO 3 MM (⅛ IN) SLICES
- SESAME OIL, FOR GREASING

SPICY PORK MARINADE

- 1 NASHI OR ASIAN PEAR, CORED
- ½ ONION
- 5 GARLIC CLOVES, PEELED
- 5 CM (2 IN) PIECE OF GINGER, PEELED
- 1 SPRING ONION (SCALLION)
- 2 TABLESPOONS SOY SAUCE
- 1 TABLESPOON CASTER (SUPERFINE) SUGAR
- 1 TABLESPOON KOREAN RICE SYRUP (SSALYEOT) OR CORN SYRUP, GLUCOSE OR HONEY
- 1 TABLESPOON SESAME OIL
- 70 G (¼ CUP) GOCHUJANG
- 2 TABLESPOONS GOCHUGARU

To make the marinade, combine all the ingredients in a food processor and blend to a puree.

Put the sliced pork in a large bowl and pour over the marinade. Using your hands, mix everything together until the pork is well coated. Cover with plastic wrap and leave to marinate in the fridge for at least 30 minutes.

Prepare a chargrill barbecue or set a chargrill pan over high heat. Working in batches, grill the pork belly for 2–3 minutes, until caramelised on both sides.

Serve immediately.

Grilled barbecued pork belly

Samgyeopsal gui

When you're having a Korean barbecue dinner party, this is a good mix-and-match with the very hot Daeji bulgogi (page 166) for any diners who are not huge fans of extreme spice. That bit of fat in the pork belly will turn to caramelised crispiness. This is fun served san choy bau–style, wrapped in crisp lettuce leaves; but, of course, it can be eaten with rice and banchan as part of a dinner feast.

SERVES 4–6

- 2 HEADS COS (ROMAINE) LETTUCE, LEAVES WASHED AND DRAINED
- 100 G (3½ OZ) PERILLA LEAVES
- 6 GARLIC CLOVES, THINLY SLICED
- 2 GREEN CHILLIES, THINLY SLICED
- 1.5 KG (3 LB 5 OZ) SKINLESS PORK BELLY, CUT INTO 3 MM (⅛ IN) SLICES
- SPICY DIPPING SAUCE (PAGE 222), TO SERVE
- SALT AND PEPPER DIPPING SAUCE (PAGE 227), TO SERVE
- SESAME OIL, FOR GREASING

Set up a Korean barbecue grill plate on a portable gas stove in the centre of the dining table.

Arrange all the fresh ingredients, pork belly and sauces on separate plates and in bowls and place them next to the grill.

Heat the grill plate until it is smoking hot, then brush the hot plate with some sesame oil. Grill the pork belly on the hot plate for 2 minutes on each side, until cooked and slightly browned.

Wrap one or two pieces of pork belly in lettuce and perilla leaves, then top with sliced garlic and chilli and your choice of sauces.

NOTE / If you do not have a Korean barbecue grill plate, just grill the pork belly on the barbecue or in a chargrill pan, then serve as above.

Braised snapper with radish

Domi mu jorim

I've chosen snapper here, as it's widely available and mild flavoured, but this can be made with just about any fish, and mackerel is the more traditional choice. The stronger taste of mackerel can be a little too much for some (it's bony, too!) and the smell can linger in the house. But it's packed with great omega-3s, so, if you love a good intense fish flavour, give the mackerel a go!

SERVES 2

- 1 WHOLE SNAPPER, SCALED AND GUTTED (ASK YOUR FISHMONGER TO DO THIS FOR YOU)
- 500 G (1 LB 2 OZ) KOREAN RADISH OR DAIKON, PEELED
- 1 × QUANTITY SPICY SOY AND SPRING ONION SAUCE (PAGE 223)
- 2 CM (¾ IN) PIECE OF GINGER, PEELED AND THINLY SLICED
- 1 SPRING ONION (SCALLION), SHREDDED INTO THIN STRIPS

Wash the snapper and pat dry with paper towel. Place on a chopping board and make three even incisions across the top side of the fish. Set aside.

Slice the radish into 2 cm (¾ in) thick wedges and spread them out evenly in a wide-based frying pan that will fit the fish.

Mix the spicy soy and spring onion sauce with 2 tablespoons of water in a jug, then pour half of the sauce evenly over the radish. Scatter over the sliced ginger, then lay the fish on top. Pour the remaining sauce over the fish.

Place the pan over high heat, cover with a lid and bring the sauce to the boil. Reduce the heat to medium and simmer for 20–30 minutes, basting the fish occasionally with the sauce. It is ready when the radish has softened and the fish is cooked.

Garnish with the spring onion and serve immediately, either straight from the frying pan or on a serving platter with rice, kimchi and some lettuce leaves.

24H
3F/4F
CLUB ICE
2F
인클
INTERNATIONAL CLUB
FREE ENTRY
Jose Cuervo
CLUB ICE
살얼음소주
슬러쉬생맥주
과일막걸리
청량샴페인
반주시대
KOREAN SOJU RESTAURANT
고기튀김/즉석떡볶이/과일빙수
반주수육전골
숯불뼈구이
해장칼국수
KNOCK
ROOM HOF
24H

Braised tofu

Dubu jorim

Tofu is basically a tasty sponge for delicious flavours, with the added bonus of being high in protein. There are many ways to cook it – my favourite is braising, so it gets the chance to soak up all the flavoursome spicy sauce. This dish is equally good served hot, cold or at room temperature.

SERVES 2

300 G (3½ OZ) SEMI-FIRM TOFU, DRAINED

SPICY SOY AND SPRING ONION SAUCE (PAGE 223)

Pat the tofu dry with paper towel and cut into 5 cm x 2 cm (2 in x ¾ in) rectangles. Place the tofu in an even layer in a wide-based frying pan or clay pot.

Pour the sauce over the tofu and toss gently until well coated. Place the pan over medium–high heat, cover with a lid and braise the tofu for 12–15 minutes, until heated through. Baste the tofu occasionally with the sauce.

Serve straight from the pan or transfer to a serving plate. Pair with steamed rice and a few banchan (pages 190–215).

NOTE / This braised tofu is perfect for the winter months. In summer, simply drizzle the sauce over fresh, chilled tofu and serve.

Braised pork belly wraps

Bo ssam

Bo ssam is the ultimate in Korean party food. Don't be fooled by the long recipe, it's super easy and very straightforward. This is a DIY affair that creates a centrepiece and gets everyone at the party talking – spread out all the components on the table for diners to put together their own wraps.

SERVES 6–8

- 1.5 KG (3 LB 5 OZ) PIECE BONELESS PORK BELLY (SEE NOTE)

BRAISING STOCK

- 1 LARGE ONION, UNPEELED, HALVED
- 10 GARLIC CLOVES, PEELED
- 2 CM (¾ IN) PIECE OF GINGER, PEELED AND THINLY SLICED
- 1 TEASPOON WHOLE BLACK PEPPERCORNS
- 1 TABLESPOON DARK BROWN SUGAR
- 2 TABLESPOONS KOREAN FERMENTED SOYBEAN PASTE (DOENJANG)

RADISH AND OYSTER KIMCHI

- 450 G (1 LB) KOREAN RADISH OR DAIKON
- 2 TEASPOONS SALT
- 150 G (¾ CUP) KIMCHI CHILLI PASTE (PAGE 16)
- 12 FRESHLY SHUCKED OYSTERS

First, braise the pork belly. Combine all the braising stock ingredients in a large stockpot, then top with 2.5 litres (2.5 quarts) of water and add the pork. Place the pot over high heat and bring to a rolling boil. Reduce the heat to medium–low, cover and simmer for 1 hour, turning the pork halfway through.

Meanwhile, prepare the radish and oyster kimchi. Peel the radish and cut into matchsticks about 5 cm (2 in) long and 5 mm (¼ in) wide. Combine the radish and salt in a small bowl and leave to sit for 10 minutes. Using your hands, squeeze as much water out of the radish as possible, then return it to the bowl. Add the kimchi paste and massage into the radish using your hands (wear food preparation gloves if necessary).

Next, add the oysters and gently stir everything together. Cover the bowl with plastic wrap and refrigerate until ready to serve.

To prepare the seasoned spring onions, place the spring onion in a bowl of chilled water and leave to rest for 10 minutes. Drain, and shake off any excess water. Combine the spring onion, gochugaru, soy sauce, sesame oil, rice vinegar and sesame seeds in a bowl and mix well. Cover the bowl with plastic wrap and refrigerate until ready to serve.

SEASONED SPRING ONIONS

- 2 SPRING ONIONS (SCALLIONS), SHREDDED INTO THIN STRIPS
- 1 TABLESPOON GOCHUGARU
- 1 TABLESPOON SOY SAUCE
- 1 TEASPOON SESAME OIL
- 2 TEASPOONS RICE VINEGAR
- 1 TEASPOON TOASTED SESAME SEEDS

TO SERVE

- 1 SEGMENT CABBAGE KIMCHI (PAGE 16), CUT INTO BITE-SIZED PIECES
- 1 HEAD COS (ROMAINE) LETTUCE, LEAVES PICKED AND RINSED
- 100 G (3½ OZ) PERILLA LEAVES
- 6 GARLIC CLOVES, THINLY SLICED (OPTIONAL)
- 2 GREEN CHILLIES, SLICED (OPTIONAL)
- SPICY DIPPING SAUCE (PAGE 222)

Once the pork is cooked, remove it from the stock and place it on a baking tray. Cover with foil and leave to rest for 15 minutes. The pork should be tender but still holding its shape. Transfer the pork to a chopping board and cut it into long strips about 8 cm (3¼ in) wide, then slice it into 5 mm thick (¼ in) pieces. Transfer the pork to a serving plate.

To serve, set out the pork belly and all the accompaniments on the dining table. Ask everyone to grab some lettuce leaves, top them with whatever they like, then wrap them up like a san choy bau!

NOTE / You can prepare the pork belly a day ahead. Cook the pork and leave it to cool to room temperature in the stock. Transfer to the fridge overnight. The stock will set into a jelly. When you're ready to serve, reheat the pork in its stock over medium heat and braise for 15 minutes. Remove the pork from the stock and allow it to rest for 10 minutes before slicing.

Fresh

Shredded soy-braised beef

Jang jorim

This is sweet, salty and garlicky, with a hint of spicy kick from the green chillies. Truly versatile, you can serve it as a main but it's also one of the most beloved banchan (side dishes) to put in a lunchbox. Sometimes I add whole peeled hard-boiled eggs to the braise to soak up some of the flavour – they do double-duty as the best snack.

SERVES 4

- 500 G (1 LB 2 OZ) GRAVY BEEF (SEE NOTE)
- 125 ML (½ CUP) SOY SAUCE
- 1 TABLESPOON MIRIN
- 75 G (2¾ OZ) CASTER (SUPERFINE) SUGAR
- 1 TEASPOON WHOLE BLACK PEPPERCORNS
- 10-12 GARLIC CLOVES, PEELED
- 6-8 LARGE GREEN CHILLIES

Cut the beef into 5–6 cm (2–2½ in) chunks. Transfer the meat to a large saucepan and fill with enough water to cover. Bring to a rolling boil over high heat. Skim off any impurities that rise to the surface, then reduce the heat to low, cover the pan, and simmer for 1 hour. Test the beef by piercing it with a fork. It should go through with a little resistance.

Add the remaining ingredients except the chillies. Cover the pan and bring to the boil over high heat, then reduce the heat to low, remove the lid and simmer for 30 minutes.

Meanwhile, cut the chillies in half lengthways and remove the seeds and membranes. Add the chillies to the pan and simmer for a further 15 minutes or until the beef is tender. By now, a fork should easily pierce the meat and the liquid should have reduced to one-third of its original volume.

Remove from the heat and, using two forks, shred the meat into bite-sized chunks so it soaks up the sauce. Leave the beef to cool to room temperature, then transfer to an airtight container and refrigerate for up to 1 week.

Serve the braised beef either chilled, straight from the fridge, or reheated in the microwave for 20–30 seconds. It goes well with simple steamed rice, Soy-braised potatoes (page 203) and Cabbage kimchi (page 16).

NOTE / You can substitute gravy beef for brisket or shank. The longer the beef mixture sits in the fridge, the more robust the flavours will become.

Soy-braised chicken wings

Dak nalgi jorim

This is especially popular with children and it's a great addition to a school lunchbox. Whenever I make it, I like to double the quantity and keep the leftovers in the fridge – that way I have lunch or dinner sorted for the next day. You just reheat the wings and drizzle that sweet and savoury sauce over some steamed rice.

SERVES 2

- 500 G (1 LB 2 OZ) CHICKEN WINGS
- 100 ML (3½ FL OZ) SOY SAUCE
- 1 TABLESPOON MIRIN
- 55 G (¼ CUP) CASTER (SUPERFINE) SUGAR
- 5 GARLIC CLOVES, CRUSHED
- 1 TABLESPOON CORNFLOUR (CORNSTARCH), MIXED WITH 2 TABLESPOONS WATER
- TOASTED SESAME SEEDS, TO SERVE
- 1 SPRING ONION (SCALLION), THINLY SLICED

Using a sharp knife, cut the chicken wings into three parts: the meaty drumette, the wingette and the tip. Save the wing tips for another recipe or discard.

Put the chicken pieces in a large saucepan and fill with 500 ml (2 cups) of water. Add the soy sauce, mirin, sugar and garlic and bring to the boil over medium–high heat. Reduce the heat to low, cover with a lid (leaving it slightly ajar), then simmer for about 1 hour, until the chicken is tender and the skin is soft, like jelly.

Pour the cornflour mixture into the sauce and stir gently to thicken. Transfer the chicken to a serving bowl, pour over the sauce and garnish with sesame seeds and spring onion. Serve immediately with steamed rice.

Braised beef short ribs

Galbi jjim

This hearty dish is typically served on traditional holidays and special occasions, especially during Chuseok (the mid-autumn harvest festival). The slow braise brings out the full flavour of the ribs and results in super-tender meat that is falling off the bone. The carrot, radish and potato all soften beautifully in the rich sauce.

SERVES 4

- 500 G (1 LB 2 OZ) BEEF SHORT RIBS
- 3 GARLIC CLOVES, ROUGHLY CHOPPED
- 2 CM (¾ IN) PIECE OF GINGER, PEELED AND THINLY SLICED
- 200 G (7 OZ) KOREAN RADISH OR DAIKON, PEELED AND CUT INTO 2.5 CM (1 IN) CHUNKS
- 2 WAXY POTATOES, SUCH AS DESIREE, DUTCH CREAMS OR YUKON, PEELED AND QUARTERED
- 2 CARROTS, CUT INTO 2 CM (¾ IN) THICK ROUNDS
- ½ ONION, THINLY SLICED
- 60 ML (¼ CUP) SOY SAUCE
- 60 ML (¼ CUP) MIRIN
- 1 TABLESPOON CASTER (SUPERFINE) SUGAR
- ¼ TEASPOON SALT
- ½ TEASPOON FRESHLY GROUND BLACK PEPPER
- 1 TEASPOON SESAME OIL
- THINLY SLICED SPRING ONION (SCALLION), TO SERVE

Cut the beef between the ribs into individual pieces and transfer to a large bowl. Soak the ribs in cold water for 10 minutes, then change the water and soak again. Repeat this process a few more times until the water is clear. Drain, then put the ribs in a large saucepan and cover with water. Boil over high heat for 10 minutes, then drain.

Wash the ribs again under cold running water to remove any impurities. Rinse the saucepan and return the ribs to it. Add 1.5 litres (6 cups) of water, then all the remaining ingredients. Cover and bring to the boil over high heat. Reduce the heat to low, remove the lid and simmer for 1 hour or until the beef is tender. Test the beef by piercing it with a fork. It should go through with very little resistance.

When you're ready to serve, scoop the beef and vegetables into a large serving bowl, then ladle over a few spoonfuls of the sauce and sprinkle with spring onion. Serve hot with steamed rice and a few banchan (pages 190–215).

Banc

반
찬

han

NEVER JUST SHY SIDE DISHES HIDING BEHIND THE MAIN, OR DULL-BUT-WORTHY VEGETABLE AFTERTHOUGHTS, KOREAN BANCHAN ARE AN INTEGRAL AND EXCITING FEATURE OF EVERY MEAL. TELLINGLY, THESE 'SIDES' ARE OFTEN THE FIRST PLATES TO BE BROUGHT OUT. ANY TYPICAL DINNERTIME WILL INCLUDE RICE, SOUP, SAUCES, MAINS AND A TANTALISINGLY VARIED ARRAY OF BANCHAN THAT BRING THEIR OWN VIBRANT COLOURS, FLAVOURS AND TEXTURES TO THE TABLE.

BANCHAN ARE OFTEN NAMED FOR THE COOKING METHOD USED: NAMUL (STEAMED, MARINATED OR STIR-FRIED VEGETABLES); BOKKEUM (STIR-FRIED WITH SAUCE); JORIM (SIMMERED IN A SEASONED BROTH); JJIM (STEAMED); JEON (PAN-FRIED); AND KIMCHI (FERMENTED). EVEN THE MOST EVERYDAY OF HOME-COOKED MEALS WILL FEATURE THREE OR FOUR OF THESE SIDE DISHES, WHILE UP TO 12 MIGHT BE SERVED AT A FORMAL DINNER.

Sauteed fernbrake

Gosari namul

Fernbrake, or bracken, is sometimes dubbed 'the beef of the mountains' due to its high protein content. Gosari are its young stems and they can be bought dried in packets at the grocery store. Sauteed gosari is prized for its chewy texture and earthy flavour and is a favourite dish for festive holidays. This is also another popular topping for Bibimbap (page 106).

SERVES 4

- 50 G (1¾ OZ, ABOUT 2 HANDFULS) DRIED FERNBRAKE (SEE NOTE)
- PINCH OF SALT
- 1 TABLESPOON VEGETABLE OIL
- 2 GARLIC CLOVES, FINELY CHOPPED
- 2 TABLESPOONS SOY SAUCE
- 2 TABLESPOONS MIRIN
- 1 TEASPOON CASTER (SUPERFINE) SUGAR
- 2 SPRING ONIONS (SCALLIONS), THINLY SLICED
- FRESHLY GROUND BLACK PEPPER, TO TASTE
- 1 TABLESPOON SESAME OIL
- TOASTED SESAME SEEDS, TO SERVE

Put the dried fernbrake in a heatproof bowl. Bring 1 litre (4 cups) of water to the boil in a kettle and pour the boiling water over the fernbrake. Leave to steep for at least 1 hour to rehydrate the fernbrake. Drain, and transfer the fernbrake to a large saucepan. Cover the fernbrake with water, add a pinch of salt and bring to the boil over high heat. Reduce the heat to medium–high and boil for 10 minutes or until the fernbrake has softened.

Drain and rinse the fernbrake twice under cold running water. Squeeze the fernbrake gently to remove as much water as possible and set aside. Line up the stems of the fernbrake, trim off any woody bits and discard, then cut the stems into 10 cm (4 in) lengths.

Heat the vegetable oil in a frying pan over medium heat. Add the garlic and fernbrake and saute for 3 minutes or until fragrant. Add the soy sauce, mirin, sugar and spring onion, and saute for another 3 minutes or until the fernbrake has softened and most of the liquid has evaporated. Taste and adjust the seasoning if necessary.

Remove from the heat, season with pepper to taste and add the sesame oil. Give it a quick stir, then leave to cool to room temperature before serving, garnished with sesame seeds.

NOTE / Fernbrake (gosari in Korean) is also called bracken. You can find it at any Korean grocery store. It usually comes dried and is sold by the packet.

Seasoned soybean sprouts

Kongnamul muchim

One of the most popular banchan in Korean cuisine, kongnamul muchim is served with almost every meal. It's mildly seasoned, which enhances the natural nutty flavour of the sprouts, and it adds a wonderful crunch when used as a topping for Bibimbap (page 106).

SERVES 4

- 1 TEASPOON SALT
- 450 G (1 LB) SOYBEAN SPROUTS
- 2 GARLIC CLOVES, FINELY CHOPPED
- 2 TEASPOONS TOASTED SESAME SEEDS
- 1 SPRING ONION (SCALLION), THINLY SLICED
- 1 TABLESPOON FISH SAUCE, OR TO TASTE
- 2 TEASPOONS SESAME OIL

Prepare a bowl of iced water and set aside.

Combine 1 litre (4 cups) of water and the salt in a large saucepan and bring to the boil over medium–high heat. Add the bean sprouts and boil, covered, for 5 minutes or until softened and translucent. Do not remove the lid during cooking or the sprouts will have an unpleasant aftertaste. Once cooked, drain them immediately and refresh in the iced water for 5 minutes to stop the cooking process. Drain, shaking off any excess water, and transfer to a mixing bowl.

Add the garlic, sesame seeds, spring onion, fish sauce and sesame oil and mix everything together well. Serve immediately, or store in the fridge in an airtight container for up to 2 days.

NOTE / For a spicy version, add 2 teaspoons of gochugaru to the mix.

01 / SAUTEED FERNBRAKE 02 / SAUTEED ZUCCHINI

03 / SEASONED SOYBEAN SPROUTS 04 / SEASONED ENGLISH SPINACH

Sauteed zucchini

Hobak muchim

Many banchan are extremely easy to whip up with just a few ingredients, and this one's a great example. The zucchini is salted for an hour or so, but that takes no effort at all and, once you're ready to cook, hobak muchim can be on the table in a couple of minutes. It's also used as one of the toppings for Bibimbap (page 106).

SERVES 4

- 2 ZUCCHINI (COURGETTES), UNPEELED, WASHED
- ⅛ TEASPOON SALT, PLUS EXTRA FOR SEASONING
- 1 TABLESPOON VEGETABLE OIL
- 2 GARLIC CLOVES, FINELY CHOPPED

Cut the zucchini crossways into 3 mm (⅛ in) thick slices and transfer to a bowl. Add the salt and give it a quick toss, then set aside for 1 hour. Strain the zucchini in a fine-mesh sieve.

Heat the vegetable oil in a frying pan over medium heat. Add the zucchini and fry gently for 2–3 minutes, until just tender. Add the garlic, 2 tablespoons of water and season to taste with salt. Saute for another minute or until the zucchini is softened but not mushy.

Transfer to a serving plate and serve at room temperature.

Seasoned English spinach

Sigeumchi muchim

Side dishes don't come any more cleverly simple than this. Sigeumchi muchim is blanched English spinach seasoned with soy sauce, garlic and sesame oil. It's quick, surprisingly delicious and good for you, too.

SERVES 4

- 250–300 G (9–10½ OZ) ENGLISH SPINACH
- 1 GARLIC CLOVE, FINELY CHOPPED
- 1 TEASPOON SESAME OIL
- 1 TEASPOON TOASTED SESAME SEEDS
- SALT, TO TASTE

Prepare a bowl of iced water and set aside.

Wash the spinach under cold running water to remove any dirt. Shake off any excess water, then set aside.

Bring a large saucepan of water to a rolling boil over high heat. Blanch the spinach for 30 seconds, then drain and immediately refresh in the iced water to stop the cooking process. Leave the spinach to chill in the water for 10 minutes, then drain and trim off the roots.

Spread the spinach out on a chopping board, then cut the stems and leaves into 5 cm (2 in) lengths. Gather the spinach with both hands and squeeze firmly to remove any excess water. Loosen up the leaves and transfer to a mixing bowl.

Add the garlic, sesame oil and sesame seeds and toss everything together with your hands. Season to taste with salt and serve right away or store in the fridge in an airtight container for up to 2 days.

DRINK
FOOD
FRESH
FROZEN

Seaweed egg roll

Gim gyeran mari

Gyeran mari, which translates as 'rolled eggs', is a Korean-style omelette that ticks the most important cooking boxes: it's ridiculously easy to make, and absolutely delicious. This popular side dish also works well in the following day's lunchbox. Whenever I have an egg roll in my lunchbox, I keep it for last so I can savour it slowly!

SERVES 2

- 3 EGGS
- 2 TEASPOONS MIRIN
- PINCH OF SALT
- 1 TEASPOON VEGETABLE OIL
- 1 NORI SHEET

Whisk the eggs and mirin together in a small bowl until well combined with no traces of egg white left in the mixture. Add a pinch of salt and whisk to combine.

Heat the vegetable oil in a 20 cm (8 in) non-stick frying pan over medium–low heat. Use a paper towel to spread the oil evenly over the base of the pan. Pour in the beaten egg mixture and swirl the pan around to spread the mixture out to the edge of the pan.

After 2–3 minutes, the omelette will start to set but the surface should still be wet. Place the nori sheet on top. Cook for another 2 minutes or until the surface is just set but still slightly wet. Using a spatula, lift one side of the omelette and fold it over the seaweed by 5 cm (2 in). Continue folding to form a log.

Transfer the egg log to a chopping board. Leave to cool for 5 minutes, then slice into 2 cm (¾ in) bite-sized pieces and serve.

NOTE / The omelette should still be a little wet on the surface when you start folding. This will help to set it into a log once it has been rolled and make it easier to cut.

Steamed eggs

Gyeran jjim

Although this isn't difficult, there is a bit of an art to mastering these savoury steamed eggs. When perfectly cooked, they should be as delicate as soft curds with a silky-smooth texture that melts in the mouth.

SERVES 2

- 3 EGGS
- 125 ML (½ CUP) ANCHOVY AND KELP STOCK (PAGE 230), CHILLED
- 1 TABLESPOON SOY SAUCE
- ½ TEASPOON SESAME OIL
- PINCH OF SALT
- 1 SPRING ONION (SCALLION), THINLY SLICED
- TOASTED SESAME SEEDS, TO SERVE

Bring a saucepan of water to a simmer over medium heat. Set a steamer basket over the pan.

Combine the eggs, anchovy and kelp stock, soy sauce, sesame oil and salt in a bowl, and whisk until just combined. Try not to fluff up the mixture too much so you get a smooth, custardy egg when cooked.

Pour the egg mixture into a heatproof serving bowl. Sprinkle half the spring onion over the top and place the bowl in the steamer basket. Cover, and steam for about 15 minutes or until the egg is just set. It should have the texture of jelly and wobble when you shake the bowl gently. Carefully remove the bowl from the steamer and leave to rest for 5 minutes. Sprinkle the remaining spring onion on top, along with a few sesame seeds, and serve warm.

Soy-braised potatoes

Gamja jorim

A few humble potatoes and some pantry staples are all that's needed to whip up this simple side dish. The potatoes are deliciously soft and soy-salty with a hint of caramelisation from the syrup and sugar.

SERVES 4

- 500 G (1 LB 2 OZ) WAXY POTATOES, SUCH AS DESIREE, DUTCH CREAMS OR YUKON, CUT INTO 2 CM (¾ IN) CUBES
- 1 TABLESPOON VEGETABLE OIL
- 60 ML (¼ CUP) SOY SAUCE
- 2 TABLESPOONS KOREAN RICE SYRUP (SSALYEOT) OR CORN SYRUP, GLUCOSE OR HONEY
- 1 TABLESPOON CASTER (SUPERFINE) SUGAR
- 1 TEASPOON TOASTED SESAME SEEDS
- 2 TEASPOONS SESAME OIL

Soak the potato in a bowl of water for 10 minutes to remove any excess starch. Drain, and set aside.

Heat the vegetable oil in a large non-stick frying pan over medium heat. Add the potato and saute for 4–5 minutes, until it turns a little translucent. Add the soy sauce, rice syrup, sugar and 250 ml (1 cup) of water, and bring to a simmer. Cook for about 10 minutes, stirring occasionally, until the liquid has almost evaporated. The potatoes should be soft when pierced with a knife, but still hold their shape.

Once cooked, stir in the sesame seeds and sesame oil. Serve warm as a side dish or refrigerate in an airtight container for up to 1 week.

Seasoned mung bean sprouts

Sukju namul

Another cleverly effortless yet flavoursome banchan, sukju namul is simply mung bean sprouts seasoned with fish sauce, garlic and lots of sesame oil. The magic here lies in the speedy blanching and refreshing of the bean sprouts: keep it quick so they retain their nutty crunch.

SERVE 4

- 450 G (1 LB) MUNG BEAN SPROUTS
- 2 TEASPOONS FISH SAUCE
- 2 GARLIC CLOVES, FINELY CHOPPED
- 1 SPRING ONION (SCALLION), THINLY SLICED
- 1 TABLESPOON SESAME OIL
- 1 TEASPOON TOASTED SESAME SEEDS

Prepare a bowl of iced water and set aside.

Bring a large saucepan of water to the boil over high heat. Add the mung bean sprouts and blanch for 1 minute. Drain, then immediately refresh in the iced water to stop the cooking process. Leave to chill in the water for 2 minutes, then drain and gently squeeze the sprouts to remove any excess water.

Transfer the sprouts to a mixing bowl, add the remaining ingredients and toss everything together until well combined. Taste and adjust the seasoning if necessary, then serve chilled or at room temperature. Store any leftovers in the fridge in an airtight container for 2–3 days.

Sauteed bellflower root

Doraji namul

The bellflower plant grows wild in the mountains of Korea; its root (doraji) is a popular ingredient in traditional cooking and as a topping for Bibimbap (page 106). Doraji has long been used in herbal medicine to treat inflammation and allergies. The root is crunchy yet chewy once cooked, but it can be quite bitter if not prepared properly – so don't skip the salting step, which will get rid of that bitterness.

SERVES 4

- 100 G (3½ OZ) DRIED BELLFLOWER ROOTS (SEE NOTE)
- 1 TABLESPOON COARSE COOKING SALT
- 1 TABLESPOON VEGETABLE OIL
- 2 TEASPOONS FISH SAUCE
- 1 GARLIC CLOVE, FINELY CHOPPED
- 1 SPRING ONION (SCALLION), GREEN PART ONLY, THINLY SLICED

Soak the dried bellflower roots in water for 8–12 hours, or overnight, to rehydrate. The next day, drain the water. The hydrated roots should be about 5 mm (¼ in) thick. If there are any larger pieces, split them into thinner strips.

Transfer the roots to a large bowl, sprinkle with the salt and mix well. Rub the roots against a chopping board for a couple of minutes to help remove the bitterness. Rinse the roots under cold running water a couple of times, then squeeze out as much water as possible. Set aside.

Heat the vegetable oil in a frying pan over medium heat. Saute the bellflower roots for 3–4 minutes, until lightly browned. Add the fish sauce and 60 ml (¼ cup) of water, and saute for a further 8–10 minutes, until the water has evaporated and the bellflower roots have turned slightly opaque. Add the garlic and spring onion and give it a quick stir, then turn off the heat. Transfer to a serving plate and allow to cool to room temperature before serving.

NOTE / Bellflower root (doraji in Korean) is also known as balloon flower or platycodon. You can find it at any Korean grocery store. It usually comes in dried form and is sold by the packet.

01 / SEASONED MUNG BEAN SPROUTS 02 / SAUTEED BELLFLOWER ROOT

03 / STIR-FRIED RADISH 04 / SEAWEED AND CUCUMBER SALAD

Stir-fried radish

Mu namul

If you're weary of salads but have radishes in your fridge, this easy stir-fry transforms them into an excitingly tasty and extremely nutritious side dish. Korean radish (mu) is a variety of white radish (daikon) with firm crisp flesh and a slightly sweet and peppery flavour.

SERVES 4

- 250 G (9 OZ) KOREAN RADISH OR DAIKON
- 1 TABLESPOON VEGETABLE OIL
- 2 GARLIC CLOVES, FINELY CHOPPED
- 1 TEASPOON CASTER (SUPERFINE) SUGAR
- 2 TEASPOONS FISH SAUCE
- 1 SPRING ONION (SCALLION), THINLY SLICED
- 1 TEASPOON TOASTED SESAME SEEDS

Wash and peel the radish, then cut it into matchsticks about 5 mm (¼ in) wide and 5 cm (2 in) long.

Heat the vegetable oil in a frying pan over medium heat. Add the radish and stir-fry for 4–5 minutes, until translucent. Add the garlic, sugar, fish sauce and 2 tablespoons of water. Give it a quick stir, cover with a lid, and reduce the heat to medium–low. Simmer for 3–4 minutes, until the radish has softened and most of the liquid has evaporated. Taste and adjust the seasoning if necessary.

Add the spring onion and sesame seeds and mix well, then remove from the heat. Transfer to a serving plate and serve at room temperature. Store any leftovers in the fridge in an airtight container for 2–3 days.

Seaweed and cucumber salad

Miyeok oi muchim

This traditional banchan isn't often found in restaurants but is very popular in home kitchens. Seaweed is packed with umami flavour and the vinegar gives this a refreshingly sharp tang that's perfect for cutting through spicy food such as Kimchi stew (page 149) and Cheesy fire chicken (page 86). It's also excellent with cold noodle dishes – try it with Festive noodle soup (page 130).

SERVES 4

- 30 G (1 OZ) DRIED WAKAME SEAWEED
- 1 SHORT CUCUMBER
- 1 GARLIC CLOVE, FINELY CHOPPED
- 1 TABLESPOON CASTER (SUPERFINE) SUGAR
- ½ TEASPOON SALT
- 60 ML (¼ CUP) WHITE VINEGAR
- TOASTED SESAME SEEDS, TO SERVE

Soak the dried seaweed in a bowl of cold water for 20–30 minutes to rehydrate. Drain, and rinse thoroughly under cold running water to remove any excess salt. Gently squeeze the seaweed to remove any excess water and transfer to a bowl.

Cut the cucumber in half lengthways, then cut each half on an angle into thin slices. Add the sliced cucumber, garlic, sugar, salt and vinegar to the seaweed. Mix well to combine, then transfer to the fridge to chill for 20 minutes.

Serve chilled, topped with toasted sesame seeds. Store any leftovers in the fridge in an airtight container for 2–3 days.

解脫門

元祖 소문난 닭한마리 元祖
맛있는집 멋있는집
닭한마리
원할매 닭한마리
히말라야 영화촬영지
히말라야 촬영지
명인집
오복순대국
칼국수 한마리

Seasoned seaweed

Gim muchim

The ultimate emergency banchan, gim muchim needs no cooking at all – it's practically an instant side dish that works with any meal. Rehydrate the dried seaweed, then season well with soy sauce and sesame oil and it's good to go. Genius!

SERVES 4

- 8 DRIED SEAWEED LAVER SHEETS (SEE NOTE)
- 1 TABLESPOON SOY SAUCE
- 1 TABLESPOON SESAME OIL
- 2 TEASPOONS TOASTED SESAME SEEDS

Stack the seaweed sheets together, tear them into small pieces, then place them in a bowl.

Add the remaining ingredients and use your hands to mix everything together until well combined. Gradually all the moisture will be absorbed by the seaweed. Loosen up the mixture if the seaweed sticks together in a big clump. Transfer to a serving plate and serve at room temperature.

Store any leftovers in the fridge in an airtight container for up to 1 week.

NOTE / Dried seaweed laver, or doljaban in Korean, is very similar to nori (seaweed) sheets, which are used to make Korean sushi rolls (page 114). Doljaban is usually thicker and coarser, which is why it is used in salads. You can find it at any Asian grocery store.

Spicy cucumber salad

Oi muchim

Refreshingly cool, yet tingling–spicy on the tastebuds, this is a great banchan for summer and pairs well with cold noodle soups such as Janchi guksu (page 130) or Naengmyeon (page 126). It's a dish that's best made fresh and enjoyed on the same day.

SERVES 4

- 2 SHORT CUCUMBERS
- 2 TEASPOONS GOCHUGARU
- 2 GARLIC CLOVES, FINELY CHOPPED
- 1 TEASPOON FISH SAUCE
- 1 TEASPOON SESAME OIL
- ½ SPRING ONION (SCALLION), THINLY SLICED
- 1 TEASPOON TOASTED SESAME SEEDS

Cut the cucumbers in half lengthways, then cut each half on an angle into thin slices. Combine the cucumber slices in a bowl with the remaining ingredients. Toss everything together with your hands until well combined. Taste and adjust the seasoning if necessary.

Transfer to a serving bowl and leave to sit for 1 hour to allow the flavours to develop. Serve at room temperature.

Stir-fried fish cake

Eomuk bokkeum

This quick stir-fry is a favourite staple in many homes – salty and sweet, a little chewy but tender. Eomuk (Korean fish cakes) are made of a compressed mixture of fish, prawns (shrimp) and squid. Traditionally thin rectangles, they now come in all different shapes and sizes, but it's best to use the sheets here and save the balls and rolls for noodle soups. Blanching quickly in boiling water removes any excess oil and softens them up.

SERVES 4

- 200 G (7 OZ) PIECE OF KOREAN FISH CAKE, THINLY SLICED
- 1 TABLESPOON VEGETABLE OIL
- 1 TABLESPOON SOY SAUCE
- 2 TEASPOONS FISH SAUCE
- 2 TEASPOONS CASTER (SUPERFINE) SUGAR
- 1 TABLESPOON MIRIN
- 1 GARLIC CLOVE, FINELY CHOPPED
- 1 SPRING ONION (SCALLION), THINLY SLICED
- 1 TEASPOON TOASTED SESAME SEEDS
- 1 TEASPOON SESAME OIL

Place the sliced fish cake in a heatproof bowl and cover with boiling water for 1 minute. Drain, then set aside.

Heat the vegetable oil in a frying pan over medium–high heat. Add the sliced fish cake and fry for 1–2 minutes, until lightly browned.

Add the soy sauce, fish sauce, sugar, mirin, garlic and spring onion and fry for another 2 minutes, until the garlic is fragrant and the sauce has almost evaporated. Remove from the heat, add the toasted sesame seeds and sesame oil, and give it a quick stir. Transfer to a serving plate.

Serve warm or at room temperature. Store any leftovers in the fridge in an airtight container for up to 1 week. Reheat before serving.

NOTE / You can make a spicy version of this dish by adding 1-2 tablespoons gochujang to the sauce.

01 / SEASONED SEAWEED 02 / SPICY CUCUMBER SALAD 03 / STIR-FRIED FISH CAKE

100% 통참깨
고소한
참기름
03
02

Sauces Condim

&

ents

SAUCES AND CONDIMENTS AREN'T EVER LEFT TO LANGUISH IN THE PANTRY CUPBOARD – THEY ARE INTEGRAL TO KOREAN CUISINE AND ESSENTIAL FOR CREATING THOSE BIG PUNCHY FLAVOURS. THERE'S A SAUCE TO ENHANCE EVERY FOOD AND EVERY COOKING STYLE. A SIMPLE BIBIM SAUCE (PAGE 220) IS ALL YOU NEED TO STIR THROUGH YOUR BIBIMBAP (PAGE 106) BEFORE EATING, BUT DON'T FORGET ITS VERSATILITY AS A SPICY CONDIMENT.

THINNER DIPPING SAUCES ARE PERFECT WITH DUMPLINGS, SASHIMI AND CRISPY FRIED SNACKS SUCH AS PAJEON (PAGE 78). WHILE FERMENTED SOYBEAN SSAMJANG 'WRAP SAUCE' IS THICK LIKE A PASTE, WHICH IS GREAT FOR FOOD THAT IS SERVED WRAPPED IN LEAVES, SAN CHOY BAU–STYLE, BECAUSE IT WON'T DRIBBLE AND DRIP ONTO YOUR CLOTHES!

THERE ARE NO RULES HERE; NO RIGHT OR WRONG CHOICES OF WHICH SAUCE GOES BEST WITH WHAT DISH. NOW'S THE TIME TO GET MIXING AND DISCOVER YOUR OWN EXCITING FAVOURITES.

Bibim sauce

Bibimjang

Because bibim sauce is mainly used for Bibimbap (page 106), it's easy to overlook that it's also a very versatile chilli sauce. There's nothing to stop you adding it to other dishes, whenever you feel like dialling up the spice.

MAKES ABOUT 200 ML (7 FL OZ)
135 G (½ CUP) GOCHUJANG
2 TABLESPOONS SESAME OIL
1 TABLESPOON CASTER (SUPERFINE) SUGAR
1 TEASPOON WHITE VINEGAR
1 GARLIC CLOVE, FINELY CHOPPED

Combine all the ingredients in a small bowl and stir until the sugar has dissolved.

Store in an airtight container in the fridge for up to 2 weeks.

In addition to bibimbap, use this sauce as a condiment for Sashimi rice bowl (page 113) and other dishes.

Spicy seafood sauce

Chojang

Chojang – made with honey, vinegar and chilli – is a sweet and tangy spicy sauce that's a perfect match for seafood dishes. It's also a great alternative to the traditional wasabi and soy dipping sauce for sashimi, so I like to serve it with Hoedeopbap (page 113).

MAKES 250 ML (1 CUP)

- 135 G (½ CUP) GOCHUJANG
- 60 ML (¼ CUP) RICE VINEGAR
- 1 TABLESPOON CASTER (SUPERFINE) SUGAR
- 2 TABLESPOONS HONEY
- 2 GARLIC CLOVES, CRUSHED
- 2 TEASPOONS SESAME OIL

Combine all the ingredients in a small bowl and stir until the sugar has dissolved.

Store in an airtight container in the fridge for up to 2 weeks.

Spicy dipping sauce

Ssamjang

Ssamjang translates to 'wrap sauce' and this thick, spicy paste won't drip and drizzle out when used as a condiment for leaf-wrapped dishes such as Bo ssam (page 176) and Barbecued beef short ribs (page 163). The addition of doenjang (fermented soybean paste) gives the sauce an umami punch that elevates meat flavours to new heights.

MAKES 125 ML (½ CUP)

- 60 G (¼ CUP) KOREAN FERMENTED SOYBEAN PASTE (DOENJANG)
- 2 TABLESPOONS GOCHUJANG
- 1 GARLIC CLOVE, CRUSHED
- 1 TEASPOON CASTER (SUPERFINE) SUGAR
- 2 TEASPOONS SESAME OIL
- 2 TEASPOONS TOASTED SESAME SEEDS

Combine all the ingredients in a small bowl and stir until the sugar has dissolved.

Store in an airtight container in the fridge for up to 2 weeks.

Spicy soy and spring onion sauce

Yangnyeomjang

Incredibly quick and easy to make, this soy-based sauce with garlic and spring onions is the essence of versatility. It works as a dressing, dipping sauce and marinade for tofu, vegetables, meat, dumplings and noodles. Once you've discovered it, you'll want to keep a batch in the fridge at all times.

MAKES ABOUT 190 ML (6½ FL OZ)

- 60 ML (¼ CUP) SOY SAUCE
- 2 TABLESPOONS RICE (OR WHITE) VINEGAR
- 6 GARLIC CLOVES, CRUSHED
- 2 TEASPOONS CASTER (SUPERFINE) SUGAR
- 2 TABLESPOONS GOCHUGARU
- ½ TEASPOON FRESHLY GROUND BLACK PEPPER
- 2-3 SPRING ONIONS (SCALLIONS), THINLY SLICED

Combine all the ingredients in a small bowl and stir until the sugar has dissolved.

Store in an airtight container in the fridge for up to 5 days.

01 / SALT AND PEPPER DIPPING SAUCE 02 / SOY AND WASABI DIPPING SAUCE 03 / SPICY DIPPING SAUCE

04 / SPICY SEAFOOD SAUCE 05 / SPICY SOY AND SPRING ONION SAUCE 06 / VINEGAR SOY DIPPING SAUCE 07 / BIBIM SAUCE

Vinegar soy dipping sauce

Choganjang

This vinegary, spicy soy dipping sauce is essential with fried treats such as Pajeon (page 78), as well as dumplings, grilled meat or fish. But, to be honest, I'd dip any foods into this bowl of liquid gold.

MAKES ABOUT 100 ML (3½ FL OZ)

- 60 ML (¼ CUP) SOY SAUCE
- 2 TABLESPOONS RICE VINEGAR
- 1 TEASPOON GOCHUGARU

Put all the ingredients in a bowl and stir until combined.

Store in an airtight container in the fridge for up to 1 month.

NOTE / For those who like it extra hot, add 1 or 2 thinly sliced bird's eye chillies.

Soy and wasabi dipping sauce

Ganjang wasabi

To fully appreciate the smoky charcoal flavour of grilled barbecue meat, it's best to enjoy it with a dipping sauce that isn't too overpowering. This thinned-down sweet soy sauce with a subtle kick of wasabi is always a popular choice at traditional barbecue restaurants.

MAKES ABOUT 125 ML (½ CUP)

- 2 TABLESPOONS SOY SAUCE
- 2 TABLESPOONS MIRIN
- 1 TEASPOON RICE VINEGAR
- 1 TABLESPOON CASTER (SUPERFINE) SUGAR
- DAB OF WASABI PASTE
- 2 TEASPOONS FINELY CHOPPED ONION

Combine all the ingredients and 2 tablespoons of water in a bowl and stir until the sugar has dissolved.

Cover and set aside for at least 1 hour to allow the flavours to develop. Serve as it is or strain to remove the onion for a clear sauce.

Store in an airtight container in the fridge for up to 5 days.

Salt and pepper dipping sauce

Gireumjang

Is it a sauce? Is it a seasoned oil? Gireumjang translates as 'oil sauce' and this is basically a pinch each of salt and pepper mixed with sesame oil. It's usually served with grilled pork dishes such as Samgyeopsal gui (page 169), but it also works well with beef. You don't need much: just a light dip in the aromatic sesame oil cleverly brings out the best flavour of the meat.

SERVES 1

- 1 TABLESPOON SESAME OIL
- ½ TEASPOON SALT
- ½ TEASPOON FRESHLY GROUND BLACK PEPPER

Pour the sesame oil into a small dipping saucer. Add the salt and pepper and stir to mix well.

Repeat to make each diner their own little dipping sauce.

추청
복전함

BASICS

Anchovy and kelp stock

Dashima myeolchi yuksu

Light and packed with flavour, this is the traditional starting point for many soups, hotpots and other dishes. Despite the anchovy base, it doesn't taste at all fishy, which makes it truly versatile.

Unlike traditional meat, chicken or even veggie stocks, making anchovy and kelp broth takes very little work and time – it might quickly become your stockpot go-to.

MAKES ABOUT 1.5 LITRES (6 CUPS)

10 G (¼ OZ) DRIED KELP (ABOUT 5-6 SMALL PIECES)

30 G (1 OZ) DRIED ANCHOVIES (ABOUT 20)

Wipe the kelp with a wet paper towel to remove any dirt then place it in a large saucepan with the anchovies. Add 1.5 litres (6 cups) of water and bring to a rolling boil over high heat. Reduce the heat to medium–low and simmer for 10 minutes.

Remove the kelp and discard it to prevent the stock becoming too salty. Simmer the anchovies for a further 10 minutes, then drain through a fine-mesh sieve into a clean saucepan. Discard the anchovies.

Korean pancake mix

Jeon garu

The key to a good jeon lies in the batter. It shouldn't be too dense or too thin, but just thick enough to hold the ingredients together. Slow pan-frying will turn it into a golden crispy pancake that is still soft and chewy (but never soggy) in the middle. Of course, you could just use store-bought pancake mix – but where's the fun in that?

MAKES 2 × 20 CM (8 IN) PANCAKES
110 G (¾ CUP) PLAIN (ALL-PURPOSE) FLOUR
2 TABLESPOONS RICE FLOUR
2 TABLESPOONS CORNFLOUR (CORNSTARCH)
¼ TEASPOON SALT
½ TEASPOON BAKING POWDER
2 GARLIC CLOVES, FINELY CHOPPED
2 CM (¾ IN) PIECE OF GINGER, PEELED AND FINELY CHOPPED
1 EGG, LIGHTLY BEATEN

Sift all the dry ingredients into a mixing bowl and stir to combine. Add the garlic and ginger, 185 ml (¾ cup) of iced water and the egg, and whisk until the batter is smooth with no lumps. Add a little more water to loosen the batter if necessary. It should be thick but still runny, with the consistency of pouring cream.

Use this batter to make any of the pancakes or fritters in this book.

Index

G

H

N

R

S

KIMCHI
750g
오뚜기
고소한
BOTTLE

오뚜기
wang
Taste Of Korea
태양초
고춧가루
Spicy Sauce
오뚜기
옛날
고추맛기름
Ottogi Red Pepper flavored Oil
SOY SAUCE FOR EGG

Published in 2025 by Smith Street Books
Naarm (Melbourne) | Australia
smithstreetbooks.com

ISBN: 978-1-9230-4991-8

Smith Street Books respectfully acknowledges the Wurundjeri People of the Kulin Nation, who are the Traditional Owners of the land on which we work, and we pay our respects to their Elders past and present.

Publisher: Paul McNally
Managing editor: Lucy Heaver
Additional text: Jane Price
Designer: George Saad
Typesetter: Megan Ellis
Food photographer: Daniel Herrmann-Zoll
Incidental photographer: Haeri Lee
Food stylist: Lee Blaylock
Home economists: Caroline Griffiths and Meryl Batlle
Proofreader: Pamela Dunne
Indexer: Rachel Pitts

Printed & bound in China by C&C Offset Printing Co., Ltd.

Most of the recipes in this book were first published in *Little Korea* in 2018, by Smith Street Books.

Book 371
10 9 8 7 6 5 4 3 2 1